1959

THE LAYMAN'S BIBLE COMMENTARY

THE LAYMAN'S BIBLE COMMENTARY
IN TWENTY-FIVE VOLUMES

THE LAYMAN'S
BIBLE COMMENTARY

Balmer H. Kelly, *Editor*

Donald G. Miller   *Associate Editors*   Arnold B. Rhodes

Dwight M. Chalmers, *Editor, John Knox Press*

VOLUME 14

THE BOOK OF
HOSEA

THE BOOK OF
JOEL

THE BOOK OF
AMOS

THE BOOK OF
OBADIAH

THE BOOK OF
JONAH

Jacob M. Myers

JOHN KNOX PRESS

RICHMOND, VIRGINIA

Published in Great Britain by SCM Press Ltd., London.

743736 80

Seventh printing 1973

International Standard Book Number (complete set): 0-8042-3026-9
International Standard Book Number (this volume): 0-8042-3014-5
Library of Congress Catalog Card Number: 59-10454
Printed in the United States of America

PREFACE

The LAYMAN'S BIBLE COMMENTARY is based on the conviction that the Bible has the Word of good news for the whole world. The Bible is not the property of a special group. It is not even the property and concern of the Church alone. It is given to the Church for its own life but also to bring God's offer of life to all mankind—wherever there are ears to hear and hearts to respond.

It is this point of view which binds the separate parts of the LAYMAN'S BIBLE COMMENTARY into a unity. There are many volumes and many writers, coming from varied backgrounds, as is the case with the Bible itself. But also as with the Bible there is a unity of purpose and of faith. The purpose is to clarify the situations and language of the Bible that it may be more and more fully understood. The faith is that in the Bible there is essentially one Word, one message of salvation, one gospel.

The LAYMAN'S BIBLE COMMENTARY is designed to be a concise non-technical guide for the layman in personal study of his own Bible. Therefore, no biblical text is printed along with the comment upon it. This commentary will have done its work precisely to the degree in which it moves its readers to take up the Bible for themselves.

The writers have used the Revised Standard Version of the Bible as their basic text. Occasionally they have differed from this translation. Where this is the case they have given their reasons. In the main, no attempt has been made either to justify the wording of the Revised Standard Version or to compare it with other translations.

The objective in this commentary is to provide the most helpful explanation of fundamental matters in simple, up-to-date terms. Exhaustive treatment of subjects has not been undertaken.

In our age knowledge of the Bible is perilously low. At the same time there are signs that many people are longing for help in getting such knowledge. Knowledge of and about the Bible is, of course, not enough. The grace of God and the work of the Holy Spirit are essential to the renewal of life through the Scriptures. It is in the happy confidence that the great hunger for the Word is a sign of God's grace already operating within men, and that the Spirit works most wonderfully where the Word is familiarly known, that this commentary has been written and published.

THE EDITORS AND
THE PUBLISHERS

THE BOOK OF

HOSEA

INTRODUCTION

Authorship and Date

There is no doubt that Hosea was the author of the book that bears his name, though some of the material about the prophet himself may come from one of his disciples or from the compiler of the book, as is possibly the case with parts of chapters 1-3. But certainly the rest of the book is a collection of "oracles" or "messages" from Hosea with perhaps an occasional addition, making application to Judah. To say that Hosea was the author does not mean, of course, that he *wrote* the book. The prophetic books were not usually written by the prophets themselves; they were composed by disciples or scribes who collected the messages which the prophets had delivered orally. The same was true in the case of our Lord, who did not write anything himself —so far as we know—but whose sayings, teachings, and deeds, as remembered by his disciples, were recorded by others.

The compilation of the messages of Hosea must have taken place soon after their delivery, possibly even during the lifetime of the prophet himself, because the book contains relatively few interpretations or applications. The longer such oracles would circulate in oral form, or the further removed from the actual period of their proclamation, the more probable it would be that such material would be expanded.

We know, moreover, that Hosea preached during the final years of the Northern Kingdom and in its capital, and when it fell and Samaria was destroyed by the Assyrian armies, its literature was taken to Judah where it was incorporated into the growing body of historical and religious literature of Israel as a whole. In the case of such a book as that of Hosea, this means that it must have been well fixed, at least in oral form, before its transmission, so as to maintain its identity. Specific dates for the separate messages themselves will be suggested in connection with the discussion of the historical situation.

Historical Situation

It is noted in the commentary that, according to the introductory verse of the book, Hosea's activity spanned the reigns of
Uzziah (783-742 B.C.), Jotham (750-735 B.C.), Ahaz (735-
715 B.C.), and Hezekiah (715-687 B.C.), all kings of Judah. So
far as the kingdom of Israel is concerned, only one king is
named, Jeroboam II (786-746 B.C.). The reference to the kings
of Judah was, in all probability, based on Isaiah 1:1, and was intended to point out to readers in Judah that Hosea was a contemporary of their own great prophet, Isaiah. The limitation of
his recorded activity to the reign of Jeroboam II may be due to
the fact that Jeroboam was the last great king of Israel and as
such was the only one comparable to the kings of Judah, especially Uzziah and Hezekiah. In addition, he was undoubtedly the
one best known in the south. However that may be, it is certain
that Hosea's prophecies extended beyond the reign of Jeroboam,
though the dynasty of Jehu, with Jeroboam II third in the line of
descent, was still in power when Hosea began his ministry (1:4).

Summarizing the historical events of the period is not easy
because the situation is a complicated one. The Syrian wars
which occupied so much time in the ninth century B.C. were
brought to an end by Joash (801-786 B.C.; see II Kings 13:25)
and Jeroboam II (II Kings 14:25-28), largely because at that
time the Arameans had been weakened by the westward thrusts
of the Assyrians, beginning with Shalmaneser III (859-824 B.C.)
and continuing under Adad-nirari III (810-783 B.C.), both of
whom conducted devastating campaigns into Palestine and Syria,
though not without serious repercussions on their own economy.
That was the real reason for the successes of Joash and Jeroboam
and the evident prosperity and peace in Israel. Amos and Hosea
both saw that Israel was enjoying only an Indian summer and
nothing permanent. The people and king, however, acted as if
their happy situation would last indefinitely. They were impressed
by material advances, and failed to take account of the eternal
verities of the Covenant upon which Israel's existence was predicated. Judgment, righteousness, brotherhood, and even God were
forgotten or were interpreted in the light of diplomatic expedien-
cies. Against this situation both prophets revolted.

When Tiglath-pileser III (745-727 B.C.) came to the throne of
Assyria the whole political situation suddenly changed. He was

one of the most powerful of the Assyrian monarchs and in a series of mighty conquests swept everything before him. He laid territory after territory under tribute, among them being that of Menahem in 738 B.C. (II Kings 15:19b). Meanwhile a coalition was organized by Rezin, king of Aram (Syria), to withstand the onslaught of the Assyrians, as Benhadad had done in the preceding century. Israel under Pekah (737-732 B.C.) was the other member of the coalition which in 733 B.C., after negotiations failed, moved against Judah to force her to join in resisting the Assyrians. According to Isaiah 7:1-6 they had already undertaken their campaign, the final aim of which was to overthrow Ahaz and place on the throne of Judah the "son of Tabeel," a Judean but the son of a woman from Tabeel, a desert principality somewhere north of Gilead.

Ahaz, however, made a deal with Tiglath-pileser III, who was probably already somewhere in northern Syria. He immediately marched against Israel from the north and divested her of her northern and eastern provinces (II Kings 15:29), took numerous captives, and was instrumental in overthrowing Pekah and putting Hoshea on the throne of a much reduced Israel. After Israel had been laid low, Damascus was conquered in 732 B.C. (II Kings 16).

For some years afterward Hoshea continued in fealty to Assyria, but after Tiglath-pileser's death in 727 B.C. he formed a kind of alliance with Egypt and withheld tribute from Assyria (II Kings 17:4). As the prophet Hosea intimated (7:8, 16; 12:1), such a course could only make matters worse; return to the Lord God was their only hope. But politics and diplomacy—all external matters—had become the national god, powerless to save but powerful to ruin. As a result of the "silly dove" diplomacy of Israel, Shalmaneser V (727-722 B.C.) pounced upon her like a hungry cat, and she never escaped again from his jaws. Samaria fell in 721 B.C. and its citizens were exiled. It is altogether likely that Hosea's activity came to an end shortly before that tragic event.

The Literary Formation of the Book

With few exceptions, our present Book of Hosea consists of poetic oracles of great beauty and virility. Although the original text in Hebrew and the ancient translations are quite unintelligible at many points, there is a vast amount of material which has been

transmitted substantially as it came from the prophet himself.
Many of the obscure or broken portions of the book would
doubtless prove altogether reasonable and sensible if we knew
the circumstances alluded to and the usage of words current at
the time.

The Purpose and Message

The purpose and message of the book cannot be separated from
the personality of the prophet. God speaks to his people through
persons and events closely related to persons. Hosea was such a
person. He was aroused to the tremendous love which God had
for his people, and the spirit of longing love runs through his
prophecies from beginning to end. And that is the message of
his sermons—God's love for Israel.

OUTLINE

The Call of Hosea. Hosea 1:1—3:5

The Date and Family Relationship of Hosea (1:1)
The Prophet's Commission (1:2-3)
The Birth and Names of Hosea's Children (1:4—2:1)
The Lord's Experience with Israel (2:2-23)
The Lesson of Hosea (3:1-5)

The Sermons of Hosea. Hosea 4:1—13:16

On the Moral Corruption of Israel (4:1-19)
On Defection in High Places (5:1—7:16)
On National Idolatry and Its Consequences (8:1-14)
On the Judgment of God (9:1—10:15)
On the Fatherly Love of God (11:1-11)
On the History of Israel's Sinfulness (11:12—13:16)

The Offer of Salvation to a Penitent People. Hosea 14:1-9

The Offer of the Lord Through the Prophet (14:1-3)
Divine Restoration and Its Consequences (14:4-8)
The Lesson of the Book (14:9)

COMMENTARY

THE CALL OF HOSEA

Hosea 1:1—3:5

The Date and Family Relationship of Hosea (1:1)

Hosea the son of Beeri prophesied in the Northern Kingdom in the reign of Jeroboam II (786-746 B.C.), a period of extraordinary prosperity (see the Introduction for discussion of the date). Nothing is known of the prophet's background beyond the fact that he was the son of Beeri and that he was a resident of Israel, as may be seen from his frequent and passionate references to "Ephraim," another name for Israel. He was a devoted patriot who deeply loved his land and people.

The theme of the book is clearly stated in verse 1: "The word of the LORD that came [literally *was*] to Hosea." The Hebrew term for "word" also means "thing," which offers a clue to its real intent; the word of God was regarded as having objective existence, even a kind of personality (see Isa. 55:11), with power to bring about the intent of the Lord.

The Prophet's Commission (1:2-3)

The prophet's commission is really the center of his message. The word of the Lord manifests itself in strange and often unlikely ways. It is always connected with a vital experience of the bearer as it is here. As the prophet looked back over his life he saw clearly that the first phase of God's word to him was his marriage with Gomer. The word of God came to him as a result of that fateful step. In it he saw the direction of the Lord, not so much for himself as for his people. The woman he married was potentially the worst kind of harlot. She was an illustration of the character of Israel, which had become a harlotrous nation, as disloyal to the Lord as Gomer was to Hosea.

When the prophet set down the experiences of his career he saw clearly the hand of God directing him to his commission. He married Gomer, the daughter of Diblaim, who conceived and bore him children whose names became symbolic of the situation and condition of Israel in his time.

The Birth and Names of Hosea's Children (1:4—2:1)

"Jezreel" (1:4-5)

At the command of the Lord, the first child was to be called Jezreel, the name of a small town some twenty miles northeast of Samaria which lent its name to the whole fertile valley in which it was located. It was known also as the country residence of the kings of Israel, where Naboth's vineyard was located (I Kings 21:1) and where Jehu put an end to the dynasty of Omri (II Kings 9). Jezreel, meaning "God sows," was thus the symbol of judgment on evildoers. But just as Jehu had been the instrument of punishment for the evil of Ahab and Jezebel, so the instrument itself would come to grief: the bloody vengeance wrought at Jezreel by Jehu was about to issue in a similar fate for his descendants, and at the same place.

Jezreel was more of a symbol than a pure historical reality; as "Armageddon" became later. It was originally the battlefield of Palestine where many national and international decisions were made, and was thus used by the prophet to point to the judgment of God, or the decision of God, for Israel. The military power of the nation will be broken "on that day" (1:5) and the vaunted prosperity of the people brought to a speedy end. The result of sin is "Jezreel"—the judgment of God.

"Not Pitied" (1:6-7)

Without indication of the lapse of time or condition, note is taken of a second child whose name is likewise symbolic—"Not pitied," which is a rather weak rendering of the Hebrew. It means "unloved" or "disliked." The name of the child signifies the breach of the Covenant love which existed between God and Israel, so that the latter now stood in the position of a rejected child. The attitude and acts of the nation had created a rupture in her relationship with God. She had rejected herself, made herself unloved by the God who had redeemed her. It was impossible for the Lord to exercise his steadfast love any further or even to forgive the people who had cut themselves off from him. Where there is no love there is no trust, and where trust is lacking there can be no real meeting, and hence no request for forgiveness. Forgiveness is never automatic.

"Not My People" (1:8-9)

The name of the third child goes a step further in that it symbolizes the completeness and finality of the breach. "Not my people" is the inevitable issue of the nation's rejection of God. The essential terms of the Covenant were "I will be your God, and you shall be my people" (Jer. 7:23). By their wanton acts the people demonstrated their unwillingness to follow the commandments of the Lord, which meant nothing less than a refusal to recognize him as their God. "Jezreel" (defection, a falling away, from God), "Unloved" (rejection of his love), and "Not my people" (dissolution of the Covenant) are thus symbolic of the nation's progressive deterioration which could end only in ultimate self-destruction.

The Salvation of the Lord (1:10—2:1)

Love never gives up. Hosea, as we shall see later, is possessed of a hope which surmounts difficulties. In his personal experience he never could divorce and forget his wayward wife. The same attitude is transferred here to the Lord, who goes to the limit in reclaiming his erring people. His hope and determination are effectively expressed in 1:10—2:1. Instead of the destruction of Israel there will be salvation, though the way may be long and hard, as subsequent developments proved. Salvation thus comes about through purification of the people by God himself. Afterward there will be growth and expansion for the people, and at the very place where they were rejected they will one day be accepted as "Sons of the living God." Their name will be changed from "Not my people" to that of "Sons of the living God." Moreover, the division between Judah and Israel will be healed and Jezreel—"place of judgment"—will become the harbinger of a new day and a new relationship as Jezreel—"God sows." The Apostle Paul's application of these verses in a different context is most instructive (Rom. 9:25-26). Observe also that he associates them with the words of Hosea 2:23.

Such flashes of hope as are found here belong to the very essence of Israel's religion. The proclamations of the prophets had but one purpose—the renewal of vital Covenant fellowship with God or, to put it another way, the calling forth of repentance. They believed in a *living God* dealing with a *living people;* and though the framework of their message was always contemporary, the fundamentals never changed.

The Lord's Experience with Israel (2:2-23)

The Sin of Israel and Its Results (2:2-13)

This whole section reads like the report of a marriage counselor. The prophet and his circle, as representatives of the Lord, are urged to plead for a reconciliation. The terminology is that of the court, as the very word "plead" or "argue" suggests. It means to take action in court. The Covenant-marriage has been voided in fact, if not in law, by the harlotry of the nation.

Something of the tenderness of the prophet stands out here rather conspicuously. Just as he obviously pleaded for his wife to remove the impediments to their marriage, he conceives of the Lord pleading with Israel to "put away her harlotry . . . and her adultery" (vs. 2). Everybody in Israel knew what harlotry and adultery did to the family and, judging by the laws against them, condemned both. But they were not so concerned about religious harlotry and adultery. Hence the prophet pleads with his people to recognize their sin of apostasy and remove it.

Unless there is a change of attitude, the outcome is inevitable. Where wholehearted reconciliation fails to take place, there is only one thing to do—to go through with the divorce proceedings. The procedure outlined here was well established in the middle of the second millennium B.C. The wife was compelled to leave everything in the house of the husband because it belonged to him; even her clothes belonged to him because he had provided them. The wife was a possession of the husband and he owned everything she would normally have. Applied to Israel, this indicates that the Lord owned everything he had provided for her. Hence to be divorced by him meant utter dispossession, with nothing left but the naked body. Israel then will be only "a wilderness," "a parched land" (vs. 3) famishing because of the lack of rain.

Her children will also be disowned because they were not the Lord's (vs. 4). The nation had even gone so far as to credit her false gods as her benefactors. That, of course, is a telling reference to the current paganizing of the religion of the Lord. It was the Lord and not Baal who had given her bread, water, wool, flax, oil, and drink (vs. 5). What came actually from God was wrongly attributed to the beneficence of her promiscuous lovers. In verse 5 there is a provocative statement of the perversion of religion. It sets forth the nation's perverse conception of the origin of her blessings and indicates the determination of the people to persist in their misguided views, despite the warning of bitter consequences. "I will go after my lovers" speaks volumes.

But the Lord had not yet spoken his final word. Israel's determination called forth God's equally resolute will that self-deception could not be allowed to prevail. Her way will ultimately be blocked, her paths will lead into a labyrinth out of which she will be unable to find her way. In short, frustrations will meet her at every turn (vs. 6). Yet her passions, fired by the lustful prosperity of the age, propel her ever further into futility. There is no abiding satisfaction in her life. She pursues her lovers but cannot claim them; she inquires after them but without success.

Once more the hope of the Lord breaks through. When she comes to herself Israel will return to him who really cares for her and with whom she found true satisfaction. "It was better with me then than now," she will say (vs. 7). Significant is the belief that she will return with the same determination—"I will go and return"—which marked her defection. Frustration compels a reassessment of her situation and will produce a change of heart.

Israel's engagement in materialistic enterprises and in pagan religious practices had blinded her to the real nature of the Lord's goodness to her. Her preoccupation with misguided enjoyments led to false assumptions. So all the blessings of life— "the grain, the wine, and the oil" (vs. 8)—were wrongly attributed to Baal, the god of nature worshiped by the Canaanites. The Lord, however, was the true giver of these things. What was more, he "lavished upon her silver and gold," doubtless gained in successful foreign commerce, which was not used in his service; rather it was "used for Baal," that is, in decorating and gilding images or temples. The very gifts of God were appropriated to objectives that were diametrically opposed to him. All this was done because Israel "did not know" that she had received her sustenance from him. That is, she had completely failed to comprehend her Covenant relationship with God.

After the expression of hope for a recognition of the true situation, with consequent repentance, the prophet's message of judgment continues. It should be observed that the prophet's conception of judgment is not annihilation, but the attempt to bring the nation to a consideration of the source of her well-being. To that end he affirms the Lord's determination to "take back" (better, "withhold") the gifts of sustenance and clothing, possibly by crop failure or the ravages of invasion (vs. 9). Perhaps that will prove to her the utter bankruptcy of her corrupt religion. She will stand naked and hungry before the very one she trusted (the pagan god Baal), and her condition will show his powerlessness to provide for her. Appeals to others will prove unavailing, for "no one shall rescue her out of my hand" (vs. 10).

Such a state of affairs will bring shame upon the nation at the most unpropitious time. For the most joyous festivals languish because the crops are a total failure (vs. 11). Observance of the celebrated agricultural feasts could not even be considered, nor could the lesser festivals be held—the new moons and the sabbaths. In other words, the Lord's judgment will result not only in a lack of daily provisions of life but in a dearth of the regular religious observances because there will be no produce of field, pasture, or vineyard to provide for their celebration. Her lovely "vines" and "fig trees" will be turned into briar patches, having been devoured or spoiled by "the beasts of the field" (vs. 12).

The Lord will call Israel to account for all her Baal celebrations which involved burning of incense by luxuriously attired worshipers (vs. 13). Her festivals were as colorful as a bride bedecked with nose ring and jeweled ornaments. With the costliest of attire—that is, with the most ornate ritual—she pursued her lovers (Baal) and completely forgot the Lord.

Promise in the Wake of Repentance (2:14-23)

Here is another of the characteristic passages of Hosea which describe the Lord as persistently striving to win back his apostate people Israel. As the prophet could not bear continued separation from Gomer, the Lord cannot endure the perpetual estrangement of his people. And because there is no sign of relenting on the part of the nation, God will put her in the position in which she found herself when he first met her. And here we have another favorite subject of the prophet—the deliverance from Egypt and the experience of the nation in the wilderness.

The figure of speech—"I will allure her" or "I am going to entice her" (vs. 14)—is rich with meaning. It refers to the proffer of freedom and a land of promise given through Moses to the Hebrews in Egypt. The Lord will once again offer to Israel the land of promise; he will lead her into the desert where he can demonstrate his grace as he did before. He will "speak tenderly" (literally, "speak to her heart") and woo her as of old. Here she will not be tempted by the amenities of a Canaanite civilization and will be brought to a fresh realization of the goodness of God. Baal had nothing to do with her former experience; only the Lord was responsible for the deliverance of the fathers from Egypt and their preservation through the bitter years in the desert.

Throughout this whole section, the Lord is the active agent. *He* acts to bring his people to a full recognition of his love for them. In the midst of the desert he will "give her her vineyards" (vs. 15), proving to the nation both his power and his deep concern for her (see Isa. 41:18; Ps. 126). The valley of trouble will become a gate of hope, thereby reversing the situation described in Joshua 7:24-26. Thus, a door of new hope and opportunity will open at the end of the vale of trouble. When Israel sees that door of hope and enters, she will respond "as in the days of her youth," that is, as she responded in the wilderness in the time of Moses. The term for "answer" or "respond" is significant, since it has several other meanings in Hebrew which are most expressive. It may indicate response, submission, or singing—hence, wooed again by the Lord she will respond to his proposal, submit to his offer, and sing for joy at the outcome of the courtship.

And when she fully understands once more the source of her blessings, she will not even mention the name of Baal (vs. 16). "Baal" was a common noun meaning "lord," "husband," "owner," and as such could be applied generally in the marital relationship. Thus "my husband" has exactly the same meaning as "my Baal." But the point of the passage is that henceforth the common term "baal" will be avoided, so that there could be no mistaking of the Lord God as a common baal. The prophet looks forward to the time when every vestige of Baalism will be wiped out and the name "baal" no longer be used of the Lord. The children will cease to be named for Baal; they will henceforth bear the name of the Lord (Yahweh). The repetition of the prophet's hope in verses 16 and 17 points up the strength of his conviction and reinforces the seriousness of his message to his compatriots. It is at once a hope and a demand to Israel.

The following verses (18-23) have more than immediate historical significance. The Lord will, "on that day," renew and extend his Covenant for them (vs. 18). It is renewal because it points in two directions—back to creation and forward to the time when similar conditions will exist. Both nature and man will be brought together in this bond, for his covenant will be with "the beasts of the field, the birds of the air, and the creeping things of the ground," all of which will be at peace with man as they were in Eden. This hope of Hosea reminds us of Isaiah 11: 6-9; 65:25; Leviticus 26:6; and Job 5:23. All nations are included in this same prophecy of a covenant of peace, because the bow and sword will be broken and war banished from the land (vs. 18). The result will be that Israel, under the protection and care of the Lord, shall "lie down in safety."

With the promise of external security through the taming of nature and the nations, the prophet turns his attention again to his people, using the marriage symbol which is central in his prophecy. When Israel gives signs of responding, the Lord will "betroth" her to himself "for ever . . . in righteousness and in justice, in steadfast love, and in mercy" (vs. 19). These are all Covenantal terms, and without the quality of life described by them there could be neither Covenant, nor betrothal, nor the realization of the Lord's promise. "Righteousness" is conformity to God's will; "justice" is the doing of the right thing with reference to one's neighbor in the same Covenantal relationship; "steadfast love" is devotion and loyalty to God and his people; "mercy" is the exercise of parental love.

Another quality operative is that of "faithfulness" (vs. 20), which is constancy, unwaveringness, and the certainty that God will never abandon his people and that they will never forsake him. There will never again be apostasy, for "you shall know the LORD." To "know" the Lord means, in Hebrew, to have intimate experience with him, such as a husband has with a wife, or children with parents. It is much more than passive acquaintance or intellectual knowledge.

When the right relationship exists between the Lord and Israel all nature rejoices in assent; nature responds actively, like a person, at the deliverance of the Lord (see also Ps. 114:1, 3-4).

So Hosea, thinking of the second deliverance, describes nature, under the control of God, responding as formerly (Hosea 2:21-23a). Each facet of nature will operate without impediment to provide for the people, the bride of the Lord. The Lord will initiate the cycle of natural production designed to feed and keep his people. The course of nature is set in motion by the Lord and not by the magical fertility rites observed in the worship of Baal. Note the personification of the natural order. The Lord will "answer" (speak to or charge) the heavens which will "answer" the earth (water and fertilize it), and the earth will germinate the grain and drive out the bud that will in turn produce the grape for wine and the olive for oil (see Ps. 104: 10-16). All of this is to take place in Jezreel, the location where previously judgment was to occur. Instead of evil and punishment, there will be good and blessing issuing from a renewed relationship of love and response between the Lord and Israel.

Jezreel will thus, according to the prophet, be sowed for the Lord, not for Baal (vs. 23). And the sowing will be in the land itself, not elsewhere or even in heaven. It marks a transformation of the land into a veritable Kingdom of God on earth which will be the dwelling place of the "pitied" or the "loved" and "my. people." For the "unloved" shall become the "beloved," and "Not my people" shall become "my people"—a play on the symbolic names of the prophet's children.

These verses set forth the prophet's hope and the Lord's promise to Israel if she responds to his appeal. The Lord's goodness and mercy go out to her as when she was in bondage in Egypt. When she is destitute and forsaken by a powerless and ruthless religion that has promised much but provided nothing, God will woo her and take her back. However, he cannot do so until the circumstances of her deprivation and hardship make her repentant.

The Lesson of Hosea (3:1-5)

The Return of His Erstwhile Wife (3:1-3)

How does this chapter fit in with the story related in chapter 1? Is this the prophet's own description of the experience of his call since it is couched in the first person? (It is to be noted that the story in chapter 1 is told in the third person.) It is possible that this chapter may be not a mere repetition of events narrated earlier but a treatment of some special feature of the experience. The latter appears likely because of its application in verse 4. The interpretation depends, at least in part, on the translation of the first part of verse 1. The following renderings are possible: (a) The Lord said to me again, "Go, love a woman"; (b) The Lord said to me, "Again go, love a woman." The former is hardly consonant with the facts as we know them from chapter 1 and would in reality make the prophet into an adulterer. The second possibility is that apparently preferred by early versions and is obviously the correct one. The prophet's family problem is traced back to the purpose of the Lord. Hosea is here urged to *continue loving* a woman, Gomer, despite her persistence in the way of harlotry. "Go . . . love" is to be understood as "keep on loving." The woman (wife) is represented as being "beloved of a paramour" and as "an adulteress," that is, one who had accepted the advances of another man. The prophet is commanded to follow the attitude of the Lord (see Eph. 5:25), who loves the children of Israel though they keep turning to other gods (lovers) and love "cakes of raisins" (Hosea 3:1). The reference is to offerings of Baal associated with the autumnal feast of ingathering when pressed cakes of dried grapes and meal were offered. The observation of the Lord's love for Israel points up his characteristic nature (see Rom. 5:8). The whole history of Israel was a trail of defection, sin, apostasy, and yet God never gave her up.

Hosea acts in accordance with the direction of the Lord and so becomes himself a word of God to Israel. He acquired the woman (legally) for the price of about four or five ounces of silver and about ten bushels of barley, paid either to her paramour or to her slaveholder if she had actually sold herself into slavery. The Hebrew indicates that she then became his legitimate wife. Being once more in legal possession of her, he promised her that she should dwell with him for many days. She must not "play the harlot" during that time. He says, "You must not be to a man and I will restrain myself for you," as the next two clauses ought probably to be translated, further stressing the hoped-for result of the prophet's reconciliation with his wife. The mixture of wooing and threats in the preceding chapter is entirely absent here. There is only the legal transaction involved in the restoration of the marriage relationship, with its insistence on the rights of the husband by virtue of the price paid for the return of the wife. The action of Hosea in paying the bridal price a second time may be intended to reflect his love for Gomer.

The Return of Israel to the Lord (3:4-5)

The deprivation of religion is compared to the deprivation of the prophet's wife. This would be particularly significant if she had been compelled to sell herself into slavery because of her infidelities. Applied to Israel, it means simply that persistence in Baalism will bring tragic consequences, even exile away from the

religious opportunities offered at the sacred shrines of the land.
That appears to be indicated by the assertion that "the children
of Israel shall dwell many days without king or prince, without
sacrifice or pillar, without ephod or teraphim" (vs. 4). Included
in this statement are all the accoutrements of the cult, and so the
reference must be to a coming period of the loss of nationhood.
The king and prince were central figures in the religious practices. And the lack of ritual implements must signify absence
from the place where they could legitimately be used. The same
may be said of the absence of sacrifice. The reference to the
"pillar" is more difficult here. The law provided that the "pillars"
of the Canaanites be destroyed (for example, Exod. 23:24), and
the Israelites were warned not to erect any for themselves (Lev.
26:1). The reference may be to memorial pillars.

The "ephod" was a priestly vestment whose use is uncertain
(see Exod. 28 and 39). The meaning of "teraphim" is obscure,
though at certain places in the Old Testament it doubtless refers
to images of some kind, or at least to objects of veneration with
which ancestral rights were associated (Gen. 31:33-35). It is
possible that in Hosea's time they were somehow connected with
priestly rites, though absolutely abhorred by earlier and later
writers. The whole passage suggests that religion as practiced in
Israel at the time will be abolished.

After a period of purging and education, "the children of Israel shall return [repent] and seek [with desire] the LORD their
God" (vs. 5). So far the verse says nothing about a return from
exile, for the word "return" is to be translated "repent." The
phrase "David their king" is probably a later interpolation based
on prophecies which had relevance only for the kingdom of
Judah. "In the latter [later] days," perhaps when trouble strikes
or when discipline has wrought its work, they will come to the
Lord trembling with fear and implore his goodness.

THE SERMONS OF HOSEA
Hosea 4:1—14:9

In the light of his experience of the hand of God in his family
life and his understanding of the will and purpose of God for his
people, Hosea proceeds to deliver a series of discourses on the
sins of the nation, God's attitude toward those sins, and especially

God's undying love for Israel, his adopted son (children). The watchword of the sermons is the *steadfast love* of God for the nation and hence his everlasting concern for her.

On the Moral Corruption of Israel (4:1-19)

The Case Against the Nation (4:1-3)

This point of the sermon states the indictment of the Lord against Israel and its results. It sounds like the opening statement of a prosecuting attorney listing the charges against the accused and their resultant effect on society. The trial is set in the great court of nature and life. "Listen," he says in effect, "to the charge (word) of the Lord, O Israelites." For "the LORD has a controversy with [case against] the inhabitants of the land" (vs. 1). With these words the nation is summoned to the bar of the Eternal with Hosea as his representative.

Specifically God charges his beloved people with lack of "faithfulness," "kindness," and "knowledge of God." These are Covenantal terms and must be understood in that light. Lack of "faithfulness" (literally "truth") signifies the absence of stability, firmness, or candor in living under the Covenant. The Covenantal relationship demanded righteousness, justice, and love toward God and man.

"Kindness" was equally wanting. This word is translated elsewhere in the Revised Standard Version by "steadfast love." It, too, is a Covenantal term meaning loyalty or devotion, and carries with it the idea of mercy. On the conception of "knowledge of God," see above on 2:20.

Verse 2 spells out in detail the elements of the indictment in terms that are vividly descriptive of the breaches of the Covenant. "Swearing" and "lying" (see 10:4) seem here to be more than a violation of the eighth commandment (ninth in many denominations); there is in all probability a reference to the second (third) commandment which has to do with using God's name deceptively, in oaths. The terms "killing," "stealing," and "committing adultery" definitely refer to the violation of the corresponding commandments in the Decalogue. The breaches of the Covenant just mentioned break out on every hand. Thus the prophet's charge against the people specifies a breach of four, possibly five of the commandments.

The effect of these crimes is evident; mourning is everywhere present (vs. 3). Even nature suffers in the sin of the people (see Amos 8:8; Joel 1:10-12; Rom. 8:22).

The Irresponsibility of the Priests (4:4-8)

Verses 4 and 5 are exceedingly difficult. The passage seems to deal mainly with the people, and includes reference to priest and prophet only to indicate the fact that the nation was not altogether responsible for its deviations from the Covenant. But priests and officials are dealt with in the following chapter. As the passage now stands, the prophet appears to be warning against too serious blame of the people for their plight, and at the same time to be circumventing the objections that would be raised by the leaders against the application of his contentions to themselves. It appears that while Hosea is laying his charge against the people because they are guilty, he is placing much of the blame on the religious leaders whose duty it was to discern the significance of the Covenant, understand its application, and furnish guidance accordingly to the nation.

"With you is my contention, O priest" (vs. 4) confirms the fact of the guilt of the priests. The priest is accused of stumbling by day and the prophet of stumbling by night. They were the religious officials whose duty it was to instruct and lead the people; but how could they do so when they themselves were guilty of malfeasance? The priests misinterpreted or deliberately falsified the Law (see Micah 3:11; Jer. 8:8-10) for personal advantage, and there were prophets associated with the religion who likewise prophesied for gain in one way or another (I Kings 22; Micah 3:11; Jer. 5:31; 6:13; 14:14). The result is stated as, "I will destroy your mother" (vs. 5). The meaning of "mother" is uncertain, though it may refer to the capital city which was the center of the nation. And if the nation with its capital city were destroyed, the religious cult in turn would cease and the livelihood of priest and prophet come to a speedy end.

Since the religious teachers had failed, the Lord's people themselves are "destroyed for lack of knowledge." Because they have despised and scorned knowledge of God, and forgotten the law of God, God will divest them of their priesthood and will forget their sons; the normal practice of succession in the line of the priesthood will cease because the kingdom itself will come to an end. The "law" or "torah" signifies *instruction* or even *revelation* and has a wider meaning than a national code of laws.

Verses 7-8 portray the character of the priests in the reign of Jeroboam II. They increased in both numbers and affluence, because it was a period of almost unparalleled prosperity for Israel. Instead of enhancing the religious institutions, and improving the teaching of the way and will of God, they deteriorated as leaders. For "the more they increased" in numbers and wealth, "the more they sinned" against the Lord. What should have been their glory they exchanged for disgrace. (This is the probable meaning of the last part of verse 7, based upon some of the ancient versions.) Their glory was their service for the Lord and his people. But instead of providing instruction and leadership for the nation they actually fed on its sin (vs. 8), which indicates that they took advantage of their position, taking increased sacrifices for sins of the people as personal perquisites (see Lev. 6:14-30; 7:6, 10). So "they are greedy for their iniquity," that is, for the iniquity of the people by which they profited.

Punishment for Priest and People (4:9-10)

The words of verse 9, "It shall be like people, like priest," are actually a response to verse 4. In response to complaints about the people, the prophet responds that the religious leaders have only themselves to blame for the situation, for they are but reaping the harvest of their sowing. Both leaders and people are suffering the consequences of their ways and deeds. They eat but shall not be satisfied, they have committed harlotry but shall not increase (vs. 10). There is the awful tragedy of sin: it is never sated until its victim is swept away to utter doom (James 1:15). In the latter part of verse 10 the reason for their judgment is spelled out—"the LORD they have forsaken *to cherish harlotry*," as indicated by the order of the Hebrew, where the important elements are at the beginning and the end of the sentence. Here there is a contrast between the Lord and harlotry which, of course, stands for popular and paganized religious practices so strongly condemned by Hosea. Apostasy was frequently symbolized as religious harlotry. The prophet's complaint is that instead of "observing" the Covenantal regulations of righteousness, justice, knowledge of the Lord, and steadfast love, they have observed the rites and ceremonies of Baal.

Popular Religious Immorality (4:11-15)

Here note is taken of the two characteristic sins of Israel—

indulgence and harlotry—and their cause. Especially important is the fact that both were associated with the religious practices as perverted by the influx of elements from Baalism. Verse 11 is a proverb (see Prov. 20:1; 23:31-35) based on long and careful observation in a land that flowed with wine as one of its most stable products. The reference here is to the cultic excesses connected with extravagant ecstasies probably induced, at least in part, by wine. Such practices were viewed with suspicion and frequently condemned severely by the prophets. The religion of the Lord was one of responsibility and soberness, as Hosea has already pointed out, and not of irresponsible ecstasy. Wine takes away "the understanding" (literally, "the heart"), thus preventing people from acting in accordance with the best that is in them.

Why was that so? Because "my people inquire of a thing of wood, and their staff gives them oracles" (vs. 12). The reference to "my people" is significant, since it stresses the fact that though they had fallen away they were still regarded as the Lord's people. They sought oracles from *wood*, something utterly lifeless and powerless in contrast to the living and powerful God, the Creator and Preserver. It is not clear just exactly what is meant; the reference may be to wooden images (Jer. 10:3-10; Hab. 2:18-19), or to trees (Gen. 12:6; Judges 9:37), or to some kind of rhabdomancy (divination by rods or wands). Whatever it was, it was useless and impotent, and oracles sought therefrom were misleading and meaningless. But a spirit of harlotry had so taken hold of the people that they were "led astray" (vs. 12). They were so obsessed by the external appeal of the fertility rituals that they lost all sense of moral judgment. Under the spell of these things they "left their God to play the harlot," that is, were driven into religious adultery with its heinous immoralities.

Beguiled by the nature cults, the people sacrifice on mountaintops, burn incense on hilltops, under supposedly sacred trees— oak, poplar, or terebinth (vs. 13). The last line, "because their shade is good," tells the story. Sensual appeal, in all its varied aspects, is the determining factor of their religion. They thought they were worshiping the Lord when in reality they were only yielding to sensual pleasure, completely oblivious of their Covenantal responsibilities. No wonder their daughters committed harlotry and their brides adultery. That was but the natural issue of their cultic stimulation.

Adulteresses were severely dealt with (Lev. 20:10) in the

economy of Israel, but the prophet says that the Lord will not punish them now for their illicit acts because the blame for their conduct lies elsewhere (vs. 14). The men themselves, the fathers and teachers of their families, are guilty. They, seized by the spirit of harlotry inherent in the nature cult, "go aside with harlots, and sacrifice with cult prostitutes." The whole community is thus brought under condemnation for its deviations from the pure religion of the Lord. So much is clear from the proverb uttered in verse 14. A people without the power of understanding —that is, of discretion and discrimination—must, in the nature of things, "come to ruin." The Hebrew word for "ruin" here occurs only three times in the Bible (Prov. 10:8, 10, margin), and implies incapacity by reason of illness or lameness. Hence the passage indicates that a people without the capacity to discern the way of the Lord and follow it is religiously sick; it will die unless restoration takes place.

Verse 15 may represent a genuine oracle of Hosea adapted to Judah by later editors. If that is the case, Hosea follows in the spirit of Amos (5:5) and condemns the apostate character of the religious shrines of his day. He certainly referred to Israel under the terms of religious harlotry. Here, however, Judah is admonished to avoid the guilt of Israel, the offense and wrong against the Lord which Israel had perpetrated. Judah is warned against going to "Gilgal" and "Beth-aven" ("house of evil," a word-play on "Beth-el," the "house of God"), and against swearing in the words, "As the LORD lives" (a word-play on "Beer-sheba"—"well of oath"). If the passage was a later development with applicability to Judah, it indicates that both Amos and Hosea were not only known but read and respected in the Southern Kingdom.

Stubborn Israel (4:16-19)

Israel, until now, has been as willful and stubborn as a stubborn heifer (vs. 16). Had not Amos warned her? Had he not pointed out her iniquities and laid bare her sins? Had he not called for repentance, for a return to the Lord? Hosea too, with more warmth and fellow feeling, admonished her and pointed out the dire consequences of her actions and deeds. Since Israel has so wantonly rejected the offer of the Lord, how could he pasture her "like a lamb" in a wide place? No herdsman can lead a stubborn herd into the most luxuriant or luscious pastures if it refuses to follow him. Neither could the Lord feed his "herd" in the pastures of the Promised Land if it would not follow him.

Israel will not follow him because she is too much devoted to idols, the gods of her own making and choice (vs. 17). To be "joined" here means to be in community with, to be associated with, to be bound to the false gods and profitless worship. Here occurs for the first time in Hosea the name "Ephraim" for Israel. It is apparently a term of endearment since the prophet uses it some thirty-seven times—more than any other writer in the Old Testament. The text of the remainder of the section is difficult (vss. 17b-19). It is possible that the last part of verse 17 refers to the well-nigh indissoluble community between Ephraim and his idols, so that nothing can be done but "let him alone." Attempts to break up the union have so far ended in failure, and that will still be the case in the future. The translation "a band of drunkards" (vs. 18) is based upon the change of only one letter in the Hebrew text. It fits in well with verse 12, and describes the inevitable accompaniment of harlotry around the festival shrines. When the people are sated with drink they dive into the cesspool of licentiousness. That happened again and again, as the Hebrew indicates, and with unbelievable intensity. Moreover, her rulers love shame, disgrace, dishonor; that is, they have been so seduced by their harlotrous practices that they love them rather than the decencies of worship in the service of the Lord.

The wind or spirit of destruction has already enveloped them and in the end will carry them away to oblivion (vs. 19). The word for "wind" in Hebrew is the same as "spirit," and the prophet deliberately employs it to indicate that the very spirit of their errors will become the storm-wind which will sweep them away into the exile of desolation.

On Defection in High Places (5:1—7:16)

A whole series of subjects is dealt with in these three chapters, encompassing almost every phase of national life, involving every segment of the population. Both the leadership of the nation and its people are taken to task for their violation of the Covenant, their breach of trust in the Lord, and their wanton acts.

Accusation of the National Leaders (5:1-2)

According to Deuteronomy 33:10, the Levites were charged with the responsibility of interpreting and applying the Law. Obviously in Hosea's time the priests failed to carry out their duty (see also Hosea 4:4). It was because of their failure in this respect that the nation was in grave peril. Those who were most blameworthy, therefore, are addressed first (vs. 1). Next comes the "house of Israel," that is, free, landholding citizens, who are called to account. As the priests are called to listen, so these are urged to give attention to the word of the Lord. Lastly, and perhaps most appropriately, the royal house is requested to lend an ear. Those three groups were the dominant classes in Israelite society and held in their hands the destiny of the nation. On several occasions they acted in concert with the Southern Kingdom, where the same general divisions of society prevailed. Since they were in such a position, Hosea rightly affirms that "the judgment pertains to" them. To those groups judgment (right decisions, justice) had been committed. But they did not execute judgment; therefore God will, and they will be the victims.

The significance of the three places mentioned—Mizpah, Tabor, and Shittim—is not apparent, though they were connected with "high places." Tabor is of course Mount Tabor, at the northeast end of the Plain of Esdraelon (Judges 4:6); Mizpah was probably the one in Gilead (Judges 10:17; 11:11, 29); Shittim was the site of the Israelite camp before the crossing of the Jordan, about a dozen miles northeast of Jericho (Num. 25:1; Joshua 2:1; 3:1). They were doubtless places venerated by Israel and taken over by Tiglath-pileser III after the Syro-Ephraimitic War. The trap, or snare, the net and the deeply dug pit, had to do with religious snares by which the people were caught when they thought they were worshiping the Lord. As the outworking of the judgment noted above, these very snares will catch those who laid them as well as those who perhaps unwittingly fall into them. For the Lord will discipline all classes who are guilty. In verse 2 there is again an inkling of hope; to chastise means to correct, or to chastise so as to correct (see Prov. 3:11; 19:18; Heb. 12:5-6), which is a characteristic Hebrew conception. Punishment was dealt out not for purposes of destruction but for purposes of purification and salvation (Hosea 2:14).

The Harlotrous Spirit of Ephraim (5:3-7)

Nothing is hidden from the Lord; he knows all (5:3; compare Ezek. 8:7-18). The whole nation is brought under condemnation —"Ephraim" and "Israel" are used in poetic parallelism—because the Lord has seen through its subterfuge. There must have been a subtle attempt to clothe religious aberrations with respectability, even to the point of more or less sincere belief that what was done was done for the Lord. But the mere fact that a religious exercise is called by the name of the Lord does not make it so. Only when it is the expression of his will and purpose and reflects his character can it be said to be from him. That was just what Israel's religion did not do; it reflected the character of Baal.

The attitude and acts of the people were characterized by the spirit of harlotry to the point where they did not and could not know the Lord (vs. 4). In many respects they probably could not even tell the difference between the worship of Baal and the worship of the Lord. The Covenant had been set aside, their consciences were warped, and they could not discern between right and wrong (see Isa. 5:20; Micah 3:2).

Self-will born of a self-set course produces pride, haughtiness, and arrogance. No matter how wrong a course of action may be, the individual or group responsible for it or participating in it frequently resents criticism, becoming more and more determined to proceed with it. That was Israel's predicament; her pride testified to her face, which probably means that it testified against her. The end result will be that Ephraim will be made to stumble by "his guilt" (vs. 5). The sure issue of guilt, or deviation from the Lord, is not only staggering, stumbling, or tottering, but actual falling (Num. 32:23; James 1:15) and destruction. The last clause of verse 5 is generally thought to be a later insertion. If so, it again points to the use made of these earlier prophecies in later times, when Judah was in the same danger as Israel.

When their sin is about to yield its bitter fruit, they will go "to seek the LORD" with their flocks and herds (vs. 6). One of the favorite topics of the prophets is condemnation of sacrifices and rituals when they are substitutes for the Covenantal life with its obligations. The prophets were not opposed to religious acts as such; they were opposed to excesses which led to complacency and, in the time of Amos and Hosea, to profligacy. In every time of trouble the people multiplied the formalities of religion in the earnest hope that they could find deliverance through them. That, says the Lord through Hosea, will be the attitude when judgment falls upon Israel. But no amount of sacrifices and offerings can deliver an unrighteous and unrepentant people (see Micah 6:7). "They will not find him" then because "he has withdrawn from them." Their lives have forced him out of the relationship essential for salvation. The way of salvation and deliverance consists of an inner and vital relationship with the Lord and not a meaningless cult, no matter how beautiful and orderly.

In their apostasy, the people themselves have acted treacherously toward the Lord, but what is even worse, they have fathered strange children (vs. 7). This indicates that they have been guilty of depriving the Lord of his children, his family; their own children brought up under such circumstances are like foreigners to God for they do not know him. Here is possibly the most serious indictment of the nation in the whole prophecy. They have destroyed the household of faith, broken the Covenant of their children, and robbed them of their rightful blessings in that relationship. Such a serious dereliction of duty cannot pass unrequited. So the coming new moon, a celebrated festival occasion, will consume them and their fields (or portions). What a thought! To be destroyed during the observance of a sacred day!

Trouble in Ephraim (5:8-12)

The first three verses (8-10) of this division form a battle cry constructed in regular metric scheme. The force of the poetry is evident in the translation; it is part of an old war song adapted by the prophet to stress the seriousness of the political situation in view of the moral and spiritual deterioration of the nation. The scene portrayed is that of impending invasion. The combination of spiritual and political destruction is purposeful. The command to sound the alarm for war refers to both, the latter following on the former. Gibeah, Ramah, and Beth-aven (Bethel) were real places, but also symbolic of the places in danger and from which and on behalf of which the horn of alarm will be sounded. The peril of self-destruction from within renders political devastation from without infinitely more probable. Rumblings were already being heard from the east; Assyria was stirring (see the Introduction). The reference is probably to the threatened reprisal brought on by the Syro-Ephraimitic War (II Kings 16:5), since the towns mentioned were all on the Jerusalem road. Political reproof was bound to follow the unholy alliance between Syria and Israel which was one of the issues resulting from reliance upon self rather than upon the Lord.

But Israel was not alone in violating the proprieties of agreed brotherly relationships. It is quite within the bounds of possibility that Judah did retaliate for the attack made upon her by the Syro-Ephraimitic alliance, and that she went too far in so doing. While Judah would be carrying out the Lord's will to resist invasion of her borders, it would be wrong to go beyond her legitimate territory. Her princes were like those who moved "the landmark" (vs. 10), that is, moved the boundary into the realm of Israel. For that the anger of the Lord will blaze against Judah because she was not acting justly or rightly; she thus broke the covenant with her sister, Israel. Unlawful acts were condemned by the prophets irrespective of the guilty party. It has sometimes been said that verse 10 refers to the unsettled conditions in the land following the fall of Samaria in 721 B.C. when Judean landholders extended their boundaries at the expense of those who remained in Israel without protection or recourse. But that is probably too late for such a vital prophecy as this, which would have little meaning to the people of Ephraim in exile.

Verse 11 also comes from the same period as verse 10. The prophet is deeply moved by the ensuing events following the attack upon Judah. Israel (Ephraim) was oppressed and crushed by the punishment visited upon her by her neighbor. But although Hosea laments the encroachment on her property, he recognizes the partial justice of Judah's action, and, more to the point, the reason for the whole situation—it was simply that Ephraim was determined to "go after" his enemy (a better translation than "vanity" which makes no sense here). Briefly, this is the political background of the passage. Israel was allied with Damascus (II Kings 16:5; Isa. 7:1-2) in such a firm alliance that her leaders went the limit in opposing both Judah and Assyria, a policy which finally ended in total disaster. To engage openly in anti-Assyrian politics was playing with fire—the fire which destroyed Samaria in 721 B.C. That is what Hosea foresaw and lamented here. The officials were so blinded by their confusion of values that they could not discern the plain handwriting on the wall of destiny. Instead of trusting in the Lord they made alliances with political and military forces which, though somewhat successful in the past, would now hasten the end.

History has within itself the seeds of judgment. Thus Ephraim was being consumed as a moth consumes garments and Judah as by dry rot (vs. 12). The determined and stubborn persistence of the leaders of Israel in their ways, religious and political, was eating holes in the fabric of her existence. The Lord was the direct cause of such judgment in history.

Ineffective Healers (5:13-14)

We may assume that the same general situation described above underlies verses 13-14. Both Ephraim and Judah were involved in the crisis during the Syro-Ephraimitic War and also subsequently. The historical reference is, in all probability, to the reign of Hoshea (732-724 B.C.) who, according to an Assyrian inscription of Tiglath-pileser III, was put on the throne by the latter after the defeat and death of Pekah (737-732 B.C.). Twice before Israel had been laid under tribute by the Assyrians—under Menahem (II Kings 15:19-20) and under Pekah (II Kings 15:29). So when Israel became aware of her condition, her sickness, she "went to Assyria, and sent to the great king" (Tiglath-pileser III). Judah did the same, perhaps later (II Kings 16:7). Both nations thus appealed to foreign, pagan Assyria for help in internal and external crises, a move opposed by Hosea in Israel and by Isaiah in Judah (Isa. 7). The prophet understood what such a course meant for Israel. The Assyrian king could not heal the nation's wounds or free her from her festering sores.

In the stark realities of history, national sins are revealed in all their bitterness and tragedy. The Lord will be present in those events like a young lion, again in both Israel and Judah (vs. 14). Instead of healing there will be tearing, instead of deliverance, exile. At work in the process of judgment was more than the outcome of a political contest; it was the moral judgment of God against a recalcitrant and self-willed people.

The Withdrawal of the Lord (5:15—6:3)

Israel refused the instruction of the Lord, who then resolved to return to his "place" (vs. 15), that is, either to the heavens or to his earlier dwelling place at Sinai (for a similar idea of the departure of the Lord from Judah see Ezek. 10). The victories of Assyrian armies may have led many people to believe that the Lord had indeed forsaken them; and that is exactly what the prophet affirms. They had rejected him and hence he let them suffer the fate of their own choosing. The Lord will withdraw himself from them (or he is held off by them) until they recognize their guilt (or are awestruck by their guilt), seek his pres-

ence, and turn toward him honestly in their distress. Such a seeking of the Lord would not come, however, without some external
pressure which might bring only a formal ceremony hardly
effective unless accompanied by a change of life and attitudes.

A defeat such as Israel apparently suffered in the Syro-
Ephraimitic War might cause reflection and the hoped-for repentance and change of life. Apparently that is just what happened;
there was at least a nominal response to the early sermons of
Hosea. The words in 6:1-2 suggest the longed-for response. The
Lord may temporarily forsake his people, but not for long! Here
is a clear recognition of guilt and the justness of God's judgment
but also of the healing power and will of the Lord! The reference
to "two days" and the "third day" points to the superficiality of
popular thinking about the judgment which had befallen the nation and a supposedly easy remedy of ritual repentance. Did they
really want to "know" and to "press on to know the LORD"? (vs.
3). Or was their ready response an easy hope for the immediate
and painless return to their former prosperity and its excesses?
Something of the latter feeling seems to be voiced in the words
of the last part of the verse. The reference to fertility is plain and
the real nature of the popular desire evident. The aim of Israel
is not really to return to the Lord but to remove the specter of
inconvenience from the midst of her enjoyment, so that she may
continue therein. Such facile and unworthy repentance would not
do. God's mercy, grace, and devotion are unlimited, but the desire for mercy must be genuine and sincere. They cannot pass
over their sins so lightly.

The Prophetic Message (6:4-6)

What has just been said about the shallow repentance of Israel
is substantiated by these verses. The question "What shall I do
with you?" (vs. 4) expresses the pathos of the prophet, together
with his utter frustration. It implies the will of God to do something about the impossible religious situation into which the nation has maneuvered herself; it reflects also the impasse confronting the Lord at the moment. "What can I do with you?" is
an equally relevant and necessary rendering of the verse. What
could, indeed, be done with a people—both Israel and Judah—
whose love or loyalty was as fleeting as the morning cloud or the
dew before the summer sun? The word for "love" or "loyalty"
is a Covenantal term and sums up the essential quality of the

Covenant. It is often combined with the word for "truth," in which case it signifies true devotion or "firm loyalty." But the present attempt at renewal of the Covenant was quite short-lived. It lasted only until things stood as before the war.

Because of their misconception of true Covenant-love as indicated by their shallow repentance, God has acted in time past as now. The Hebrew word for "therefore" in verse 5 represents the statement of a fact rather than a condition or the outcome of a condition. That is what had taken place. The Lord had hewn them by the prophets. Two thoughts may be combined here since the term "to hew" means both to cut to pieces and to fashion. The word of God by the prophets was constantly at work endeavoring to fashion his people according to his plan and will; on the other hand, it was also at work hammering to pieces those who resisted it (Jer. 23:29). It had within it the power to carry out the intention of its creator (Isa. 55:11). His word had "slain them," which is another indication of the inherent power of the divine word. That was, of course, the power of judgment, which appears to have been more effective than that of salvation (see Jer. 5:14; Heb. 4:12; Rev. 1:16), though it must always be remembered that for the biblical writers judgment was for the purpose of salvation, not for destruction of persons. That, too, seems to be the thought underlying the last section of the verse. The judgments of God were given to Israel from of old and were repeated and applied by the prophets and priests with one purpose in mind: to guide her in her Covenantal responsibilities as they related to God and her neighbors.

The Covenant was the shining light by which Israel was to direct her way. That is what the Lord delighted in, not in sacrifice (vs. 6). As already pointed out, "steadfast love" is a Covenantal term and refers to the unswerving loyalty demanded by the Lord of those bound to him in that relationship. The same may be said of "the knowledge of God" (see above on 2:14-23). The Lord, according to the prophets, did not lack sacrifices and burnt offerings; these were plentiful in Israel and Judah because that was the spectacular, appealing, and easy way of service to him. It was not that he rejected such methods of worship, but that sacrifices and offerings ought to have been the expression of truly dedicated lives and not a substitute for them. Remember the observation of Jesus in Matthew 23:23.

Ephraim's Harlotry (6:7-10)

The first part of verse 7 is very difficult because of the uncertainty of the word "Adam." The whole section must be a portion of a larger prophecy, because it assumes something antecedent to the "they" which is the subject. If we knew what went before we should, in all probability, be able to interpret the reference to "Adam." It is possible to read as follows: "like Adam," "like mankind, or humanity," or "like at Adam." If we take the first, the meaning would be that they, the people of Israel, transgressed like the Adam of Genesis; if the second, it would indicate that they were guilty just as all mankind is; if the third, it would mean that they now sinned as they had at Adam—that is, at the ford of the Jordan, at present Tell ed-Damijeh, to which the dammed waters of the Jordan extended when Israel crossed into the Promised Land (Joshua 3:16). Since parallelism with the following verse requires a place name, the latter is the most probable meaning, though its significance escapes us at present.

Gilead is also mentioned as harboring doers of evil (vs. 8). The reference is equally obscure, though there may be a reminiscence of the revolt in the Northern Kingdom raised by Pekah (737-732 B.C.) and fifty Gileadites (II Kings 15:25). Again it may refer to some other event such as the Jephthah episode (Judges 11), the fact that Gilead was the mustering center for Absalom in his rebellion against David (II Sam. 17:26), that the Jehu revolution began at Ramoth-gilead (II Kings 9), or that Gilead figured in the first conquest of Israel by Tiglath-pileser III (II Kings 15:29). The charge against Gilead, which is here called a "city," is a very serious one—that it is "tracked with blood." For that reason, the whole history of Gilead may be involved in the denunciation of the prophet. Transgression of the Covenant, acting deceitfully against the Lord, and a city tracked with blood—what an array of accusations against Israel!

If the translation of verse 9 is correct, Hosea makes the most serious charge against the priests in the Old Testament. In the New Testament there is an analogy in our Lord's accusation of Jerusalem (Matt. 23:37; Luke 13:33-34), but there the priests are not accused directly. The prophet here compares the priests to bands of robbers who lie in wait for the unsuspecting traveler. The translation "they murder on the way to Shechem" is very uncertain. Shechem was one of the cities of refuge (Joshua 20:7;

21:21) and an important religious center (I Kings 12:1). It may be that the priests were responsible for some infraction of the law of asylum (Num. 35). In any case, they also committed "villainy," or acts of opprobrium.

It has been suggested that "the house of Israel" (vs. 10) originally read "Bethel" ("house of God"), which would fit in rather well with the condemnation heaped upon that shrine of the Northern Kingdom by Hosea (10:15, margin) and especially by Amos (4:4; 5:5-6). The Lord (prophet) sees there "a horrible thing," that is, a most detestable display, explained in the following portion of the verse. That is where Ephraim's harlotry and Israel's uncleanness are located.

Judah's Harvest (6:11a)

Neither will Judah escape. She is just as guilty as her sister Israel, and will reap the fruit of her iniquity in due time. The first part of verse 11 may be a later insertion, whereby a Judean editor applies the prophecy of Hosea to his own time and situation. "Harvest" here can hardly mean blessing, in view of the general context of the passage.

The Depth of Israel's Sin-Sickness (6:11b—7:7)

It was assuredly not the will of the Lord that his people should perish in their sin-sickness; his will was that they might be restored and healed (see Ezek. 18:23; 33:11). He is not only interested in and desirous of restoring "the fortunes" of Israel, but will go to any possible lengths to do so. The Bible is full of expressions setting forth the determination of the Lord to "heal" his people, no matter how desperately ill or wounded they may be. But like a physician examining the injuries of a patient, he comes to realize how deep and serious sin-sickness is only when he examines the victim. Any examination of Israel revealed the well-nigh mortal wounds which she had received from her religious apostasy. The phrase "they deal falsely" (7:1) sums up the total corruption of the people. They are corrupt themselves and therefore cannot help acting corruptly in all their dealings (see Prov. 4:23). A virtual state of anarchy exists, for thieves enter houses and bandits lie in wait in the dark places in the city and countryside. The verse reflects the unsettled situation in Ephraim in the last years of its existence, which in turn is indicative of the deterioration of the nation. Israel was beyond healing with ordi-

nary remedies; only exile could avail, and perhaps even that
would not save from final destruction.

They have gone so far that they can no longer give consideration to their ways or to the Lord (vs. 2). Nor do they understand the constant presence of the Lord and his remembrance of
their evil. There is no history with the Lord; it is always now
with him, hence all their "evil works" are before him. All their
deeds and practices surround them like a garment, so that they
are now clothed with their defections.

By their evil works they make the king rejoice and by their
"treachery" they make glad the princes (vs. 3). The whole political structure hangs together. It is "Like kings and princes, like
people" (compare 4:9). They interact upon one another to the
supposed advantage of each in turn. Secret intrigues, violence, debauchery, and shame are the inevitable fruit of their doings.

All of them, kings and people, were religious and political
adulterers; they were unfaithful to their trust and prostituted the
best interests of the kingdom (vs. 4). They failed to take seri-
ously and honestly their obligations of loyalty to the Covenant.
The comparison with the figure of the oven may be interpreted
in a number of ways, depending on the combinations of words in
the Hebrew text. The meaning of the Revised Standard Version
is that the rulers are like an oven whose heat is kept on contin-
uously except when they are busy with new plans. Another possibility is that they are like an oven continuing to heat without
the baker while he is at work preparing the dough, signifying the
ceaseless burning of passion without the normal interval. Or the
figure may mean that they are like an oven whose heat is turned
off while the dough is kneaded and leavened, in which case the
officials of the land knew just what they were about and never
permitted the oven to burn uselessly; they had their own purposes which they carried out as cleverly as the baker who never
takes chances on burning the oven needlessly. In the latter instance the figure is somewhat mixed, shifting between the oven
and the baker. At any rate, here is the figure of the burning oven
(passion for immorality in every form) and the skilled baker
(officials) who knows how to perform his work to the best advantage. The guilty rulers of Israel were passionately carrying on
their self-willed plans.

Verse 5 expresses further the pursuit of the plan. "On the day
of our king" refers to some celebration, perhaps an annual coro-

nation festival, when there were observances of various kinds together with the customary feast. There the princes were rendered
impotent ("made sick," not "became sick") by the heat of wine.
The reference may be to a conspiracy hatched by the officials
against the king and perpetrated upon an unsuspecting court (see
II Kings 15:14, 25, 30). The scene portrayed is that of a royal
banquet where the participating parties indulge in drinking and
debauchery until all sense of propriety is lost. The princes are
drunk, the king joins with the scorners, and the subversives go
to work. Their hearts burn like an oven "with intrigue" so that
they can hardly restrain themselves (vs. 6). The figure here is
slightly different from that in verse 4. There the whole crowd of
evildoers burn with passionate desire for the sake of their designs;
here the same general idea is expressed but the seat of desire—
"their hearts"—is said to burn like an oven with secret plans,
hopes, and intrigues. The celebration thus proceeded, and throughout the night their desire or passion was held in check. It waited
in the belief that everything was working according to plan, and
then when the heat of the wine had taken full effect the time to
strike arrived. In the morning the burning desire of the intriguers
burst forth into flaming wrath, consuming the gullible officials
who had so enthusiastically banqueted through the night.

The final verse of the section (vs. 7) clarifies the issues dealt
with here, and although we cannot be absolutely certain of the
details involved there can be no doubt of the over-all meaning.
The disease of conspiracy and rebellion had taken hold of the
whole nation—"All of them are hot as an oven." The spirit of
intrigue seemed to have taken possession of everybody. There
can hardly be any question that Hosea has reference to the rapid
turnover of kings during the last years of the kingdom. From
746 B.C. to 721 B.C. there were no less than six kings, several of
them coming to power by overturning the preceding ruler or
ruling party. The magistrates were devoured, their kings fell, and
both were replaced without consultation with the Lord. The people failed to call upon the Lord for assistance, they did not inquire about his will, and, worst of all, they followed their own
inclinations regardless of the Covenant of the Lord.

Ephraim, a Half-Baked Cake (7:8-10)

The rich figures of speech employed by Hosea in verses 8-10
are quite expressive of his own experience and that of his people.

In the period of the prophet it was perhaps more true than ever that Ephraim was a mixed population. There was a deportation of captives by Assyria after the deposition of Pekah and the elevation of Hoshea to the throne (see II Kings 15:29-30; Isa. 9:1). Such deportation was followed by the importation of new peoples taken captive elsewhere during the Assyrian campaigns. But in addition, the Northern Kingdom was always more cosmopolitan in character than Judah by virtue of its location.

The figure for mixing (7:8) is used in connection with the preparation of sacrificial offerings (for example, Lev. 2:4, 7), but most interestingly of the confusion of tongues in Genesis 11:7, 9. Ephraim was indeed mingled and intermingled with the peoples. Now she appeared as a cake unturned upon the hot baking stone, still "dough" on the top but burnt on the underside. She lacked decisiveness, had lost her sense of discrimination, and thus could devise only half-baked policies of political and social action.

As a result of all this, foreigners sap the strength of the nation (vs. 9). Israel wastes away because of political entanglements. The worst feature of the situation was that the nation had no longer any power of discernment: she "knows it not." The very elements which Israel thought made for strength were actually weakening her. And the time of her life was growing short: "gray hairs" have already covered the head and she "knows it not." The indecision of old age has come upon the nation without being noticed. The prophet uses the two-pronged figure to emphasize the condition of his people: the vacillation of old age and the proximity of death in old age.

Age sometimes begets an unwarranted and unsuspecting pride. The age and experience of Israel, instead of making her wise, discriminating, and circumspect, produced a spirit of conceit. The people failed to repent, to "return to the LORD their God" (vs. 10). They felt self-reliant, self-sufficient, and able to handle their problems without recourse to God. Despite the troubles besetting them on every side they did not "seek him." In the accusation brought against his people, Hosea points to the true way to security which lay in a return to the Lord and reliance upon him and his way.

Israel's Silly-Dove Diplomacy (7:11-13)

The half-baked politics of Ephraim make him like a silly dove flitting now to Assyria, now to Egypt, depending upon which way the more propitious wind blows (vs. 11). The dove is the proverbial creature of innocence and thoughtlessness. It can be easily snared into a trap by food or can lose itself in search of food when it darts hither and thither blissfully ignorant of the danger that surrounds it. That is exactly Ephraim's character in the present crisis, appealing to Egypt when threatened from Assyria and vice versa (II Kings 17:4). It is believed that there were pro-Assyrian and pro-Egyptian parties in the Northern Kingdom at this time; if so, we can understand the conflicting policies, dependent upon the sentiments of the party in power.

What is the attitude of the Lord toward this silly-dove diplomacy? When they go, he will spread his net over them and snare them as other "birds" are snared (vs. 12). The reference is to the common oriental practice of bird trapping frequently depicted on ancient monuments. Once more the prophet warns against the snares awaiting Ephraim from all sides. The latter part of verse 12 is obscure at present but doubtless has something to do with the catching of Ephraim while in flight to foreign parts. The meaning of the whole verse, however, is evident. As the unsuspecting dove is trapped by the hunter, so Ephraim will be trapped by those for whose bait he goes.

At the end of the trail of wandering lies destruction and desolation because the nation has rebelled against God, and refused the very source of security and refuge from trouble (vs. 13). The first part of the verse rebukes Ephraim for political policy, the second for apostasy. But the situation is still not without hope, for "I would redeem them," says the Lord. The term "redeem" is used in commercial law and is full of meaning here. God stands ready to ransom his people, even from the closing jaws of the abyss of exile. Yet they "speak lies" against him; they have been and continue to be obdurate. Perhaps there are two thoughts here: (a) I would (yet) redeem them, though they have spoken lies against me; (b) how can I redeem them when they speak lies against me, when they persist in their misconceptions upon which all their policies and actions are based?

Materialistic Religion (7:14-16)

Here the prophet returns to the formal religious practices of the day. When the people cried to the Lord in their need they did not do it with their whole heart. They thought they were interceding with the Lord when actually they were merely following the national cult. There can be no doubt of the seriousness of their affliction or distress, for they howled upon their couches (vs. 14). However, they were more concerned about material wants than religious needs, though they would hardly have distinguished between the two since the absence of material things was naturally interpreted as the result of the displeasure of God. Blessings indicated the presence and favor of God, while the lack of them spelled his disfavor. To implore the favor of God they resorted to Canaanite rites: "for grain and wine they gash themselves," just as the priests of Baal Melqart did on Mount Carmel (I Kings 18:28). In so doing they turned away from the Lord, who cannot be worshiped by such pagan rites.

Despite the fact that the Lord had disciplined them—for example, in the wilderness (vs. 15; see 2:14-15) and in the adversities which beset them through the preceding experiences undergone by the Northern Kingdom—they still devised evil against him. The religion of Moses was subverted by the influx of heathen forms and practices by which the Covenant was repudiated. What they did was to separate worship from personal relationships and regard it largely as a way of securing material well-being. Hence the prophet affirms that they turn continually to Baal when the crops fail and adversity arises (vs. 16). They have become like a "treacherous bow"; that is, a slack bow which looks good but has no spring, packs no power to propel the arrow. Their religion looks good, it is fashionable, efficient, beautiful, regular, but without spiritual power. It stresses the wrong phases —external expression rather than inward strength and direction in harmony with the will of the Lord. When the final test comes, the deceptiveness of their religion will be made plain. Their leaders will become victims of their own folly, for they cannot maintain themselves or their people with the power of the sword. "The insolence of their tongue" refers to the open flouting of the will of the Lord, their ridiculing of the prophets who endeavored to instruct and warn them (see Amos 7:12-13). "Their derision in the land of Egypt" has a double meaning. Seeking Egypt's help will be useless since Egypt cannot be depended upon; Egypt will come to the rescue only in response to her own designs, which rarely coincide with Israel's needs. Egypt also symbolizes exile and slavery. In the coming captivity, they will be derided on all sides.

On National Idolatry and Its Consequences (8:1-14)

The Broken Covenant (8:1-3)

This little section begins with the Lord's command to the prophet, who is to sound the alarm of war because the time of judgment has arrived (8:1). The alarm was sounded when an enemy approached a city. The enemy is now approaching like a vulture-eagle, swooping down upon the "house of the LORD" (the land of the Lord, which is Israel; see also 9:15). The message of Hosea which hitherto had been one of hope now becomes one of impending doom. The nation refused to listen, "they have broken my covenant, and transgressed my law." These were the words of the Lord which the prophet was under obligation to declare. The breach of the Covenant consisted in the substitution of Canaanite religion for that of the Lord. "My law" is synonymous with "Covenant," and has a much wider meaning than a code of laws. It signifies the teaching or revelation of the Lord against which they had rebelled, for that is what transgression here involves. It was willful, deliberate abrogation of the Covenant.

When the blow falls their memory of the Lord will be refreshed. Then they will cry to him with their lips, though with their lives and loyalty they have served Baal (vs. 2). But their deeds testify against them (see 5:3-4). Such easy repentance does not indicate the real change of heart which alone might be effective. Lives of repentance were harder to come by than words, and Israel was better at words than at life. To say "we . . . know thee" requires intimate experiential relationship which does not transpire overnight. It will be too late to enter into such a relationship when the Assyrian armies are marching into the land. The fact is that Israel has rejected the good, namely, all that the Lord had offered (vs. 3). Again and again, the prophets had urged her to seek the Lord (Amos 5:4, 6, 14), but the more she was implored to do so the further she appeared to veer away from him (Hosea 4:7; 11:2). There can be only one result: "the enemy shall pursue him."

Officials and Cults (8:4-6)

The first part of verse 4 refers to the rapid and disastrous turnover of regal families in the Northern Kingdom. In a period of about two hundred years it had nineteen kings, represented by four dynasties. Each dynasty came to a violent end, and during the last years of the kingdom there were assassinations and usurpations. The verse is a reflection on that situation. Their kings and princes were set up by others than the Lord. The last part of the verse, "With their silver and gold they made idols," may refer to the bull pedestals constructed by Jeroboam I and placed in the shrines at Bethel and Dan. Originally they may have been considered innocuous, as nothing more than stands or pedestals for the invisible presence of the Lord, just as the Ark in the Jerusalem Temple was. Later on, however, these symbols began to take on greater significance and the editor of the Books of Kings speaks, almost ritually, of Jeroboam the son of Nebat who led Israel to sin. They became images which were doubtless overlaid with precious metals. What the cult officials thought was beautiful and an effective means of worship became a snare and led to their own destruction.

Then comes the command of the Lord, "Get rid of your calves, O Samaria; my anger burns against them," as verse 5 should probably be translated. There was still hope for repentance and reform as the second part of the verse indicates—how long will they be incapable of being declared innocent? So long as the shrines of Bethel and Dan continue their illicit practices, Samaria cannot be legally innocent. The Lord's wrath is burning against those hotbeds of iniquity and he demands immediate expulsion of them from Israel. For what are these idols—nothing more or less than man-made, handmade gods (vs. 6). There is nothing divine in them; they have no power to do anything (see Isa. 46:1-2). The judgment upon the created gods of Samaria is the flame which will utterly destroy them (vs. 6, margin).

An Unprofitable Way (8:7-10)

The proverb of verse 7 puts the condition confronting the nation succinctly. They have sown the wind, that is, nothing perceptible so far as the good fortune of Israel was concerned. The harvest from nothing is precisely nothing. The formalism without morality characteristic of the religion of Israel had within it the seeds of its own destruction (see Gal. 6:7). The next part of the verse is difficult. The Revised Standard Version takes it to refer to the standing grain of the moment which will not head up; and even if it should do so, Israel would not enjoy it, for foreigners will devour it.

Aliens were already in the process of devouring, swallowing up Israel (vs. 8). For that matter, she had been for a long time in the clutches of hostile powers. From the period of the Syrian wars in the time of Ahab these alien powers were taking their toll, not in an overt manner but subtly and insidiously through religious and political influence. There was the widespread and devastating influence of Tyrian Baalism; also the compromises required by alliances with Syria, later with Assyria and perhaps Egypt. Israel was so deeply involved that to all intents and purposes she had already been swallowed up. Captivity is not simply a physical fact; it is, or at least it begins with, a spiritual condition brought about by personal or national relationships. Long before 721 B.C., Israel had been taken captive. Now "they are among the nations" through alliances and foreign cult practices within the nation. Worst of all, they are "as a useless vessel," without influence or status so far as their captors are concerned.

Ephraim has already sold out to Assyria (vs. 9). The leaders of the nation have made her like a wild ass, stubbornly, willfully determined to follow her own inclination or desire. The fact that she is "wandering alone" indicates the path she has chosen for herself; wild asses, like many other wild animals, roam in packs. Moreover "Ephraim has hired lovers" or "Ephraim has given love-gifts"—a clause with a twofold meaning. The former points to political alliances consummated, with tribute or tax of some kind as the price required of Ephraim; the second, to the bridal price which Ephraim paid for support. In any event, the international relationships into which the leaders forced the nation were unnatural, and wholly to the disadvantage of the people. Verse 10 is very difficult in the historical context because the expression "gather them" is used in later writers for gathering the exiles back to their land. However, the verb "gather" is used in Micah 4:12 and Joel 3:2 of gathering for judgment. If that is the usage to be applied here, the thought would be that though Israel has hired allies from among the nations the Lord will gather them for judgment. Allies cannot afford security from judgment for long; they will presently be gathered for the purpose of judgment. They have anointed kings and princes (see 8:4 and 7:7) of their own accord, but that practice will soon cease. Destruction is at hand, then there will be neither need nor opportunity to anoint kings. The bitter experiences of exile will put to an end such presumptuous practices.

Judgment Upon the False Religion of Israel (8:11-13)

To an outsider the religion of Israel would have appeared quite healthy and vigorous. For formalities were observed on every side and the "high places" appointed for such purposes were crowded with worshipers (see Amos 4:4-5; 5:21-24). There was no dearth of religious institutions; there was an abundance of them. Once again let it be said that many of the people must have been sincere in carrying out what they were taught. They believed, in all probability, that the altars which their leaders erected were really provided for the appeasement of the Lord and atonement for their sins (8:11). There may be a play on words here, and without changing the Hebrew text we may read: "Because Ephraim has multiplied altars for atonement, they have become to him altars for sinning." But however one may translate, the issue is the same. The formal religion of Ephraim was only a façade, and it invited a false and pernicious security.

So accustomed had the hierarchy of the nation become to its self-appointed methods of worship and ways of life that all perception of the true meaning of the laws of the Eternal had been lost (vs. 12). No amount of revelation can by itself influence an unreceptive people. Hence the prophet's remark that though the Lord shall give them "laws by ten thousands," or applications of law for every possible emergency, they would still be reckoned as strange or foreign devices. Here is an excellent illustration of the powerlessness of instruction, or revelation, by itself to save. Only where the Covenant relationship remains intact can there be the saving response of individual or nation.

The multiplication of altars and the offering of countless sacrifices were actually an expression of the desires of the nation. Such sacrifices were carried out with avidity; they were regarded as the essence of religion. The people loved them (vs. 13). They loved to consume the sacred peace offerings at the altars of the land. The sacrifices made a kind of religious picnic. But the Lord is aware of their iniquity and will permit their sins to find them out. Their sacrifices will not save them for "they shall return to Egypt"; that is, go into bondage again until they become aware of their defections and sue for forgiveness in genuine repentance.

Palaces and Fortresses (8:14)

The fact that "Israel has forgotten his Maker" is reflected not only in the consummation of foreign alliances but also in the construction of palaces and fortresses (vs. 14). Omri and Ahab had built Samaria with its host of official structures. Excavations there show enormous reconstruction activity in the reign of Jeroboam II. Such man-made feats led to a false sense of security. These things will become fuel for God's destructive fire, not so much because they are evil in themselves as because they are monuments of a misdirected faith, and can neither sustain nor preserve.

On the Judgment of God (9:1—10:15)

This sermon concerns the outcome of the course Israel has been following. It deals with the causes for judgment, its imminence, its relentlessness.

Return to Egypt (9:1-6)

The discourse was apparently delivered at some great festival, possibly at the harvest or ingathering (Exod. 23:15-16; 34:22), when a large concourse of worshipers had assembled at one of the great shrines of the nation, perhaps Bethel. Such festivals were naturally a time of festal joy and happy celebration, especially if the harvests were abundant. The prophet, however, exhorts the people to refrain from the usual expressions of joy, because of the crisis brought on by their pagan lives and attitudes (9:1). The other nations who have not had the advantage of the instruction of the Lord cannot be blamed as much as Israel, who certainly knows better. The festival being celebrated should be one not of rejoicing but rather of mourning, for Israel has "played the harlot." The threshing floor had in reality become a den of iniquity, and she preferred the harlot's hire there rather than genuine thanksgiving to the Lord for his goodness. To mix the extravagances of the fertility cults with the celebrations of the Lord was incongruous with the moral standards of Israelite religion. The threshing floor and wine press will not continue to feed them, and the new wine will prove deceptive (vs. 2). Nature will revolt against them because they have disgraced nature's God.

The cessation of the productiveness of the land will be due not to drought or famine but to invasion and subsequent exile. Hosea returns to the theme which recurs a number of times in his prophecies (7:16; 8:13)—"Ephraim shall return to Egypt" (vs.

3). The moral and religious character of the people has been so warped that reconstitution can come about only through a thorough cleansing. Of course the clause just quoted is explained by the parallelism, "they shall eat unclean food in Assyria," for no actual exile in Egypt is contemplated. What is insisted upon is that Israel must once again be brought to a realization of her true relationship to the Lord, that of a servant, responsive and obedient to him. In Assyria it will not be possible to carry out the customary rituals of the Lord (vs. 4). There will be no "house of the LORD," no sacred altar, no provision for the sacrifices and offerings which the people so disastrously perverted in the homeland. The first fruits of harvest and ingathering cannot be observed and so what they eat will appear like mourner's bread (see Deut. 26:14). "All who eat of it shall be defiled" because the proper ritual procedure has not been observed. Their food will be for the satisfaction of hunger only, without the customary recognition of the Lord. Then those who sought material benefits will have their desire satisfied, only to discover that man cannot live by bread alone (Deut. 8:3; Matt. 4:4).

Verse 5 is a rhetorical question addressed to the worshipers at the festival in the hope of bringing them to serious reflection on the situation confronting them. What will they do at the time of the appointed festivals, on the day of new moon and sabbath? How will they then celebrate the harvest festival? These festivals and seasons were appointed for the homeland and could not legitimately be celebrated in a strange land. But the reaction of the celebrants must have been negative, for immediately the prophet comes back to the threatened judgment of the Lord about to engulf them. Since they will not listen to the offer of the Lord, they are headed for destruction (vs. 6, margin—here a substitute expression for Assyria, as the Revised Standard Version has rightly translated, for Assyria and destruction proved to be opposite sides of the same coin). The reference to Egypt and Memphis is to the ancient burial grounds south of present-day Cairo over which stretch some sixty miles of pyramids, symbolized by Memphis, above which stood the great mortuary temple of Djoser at Saqqara. This reference can mean nothing else than that Israel was headed for the cemetery. The things now most precious to her will be consigned to desolation. Her prized possessions—idols, heirlooms, cult objects, even houses—will be overgrown, and thorns and briars will cover her erstwhile dwelling places.

Popular Reaction to the Prophets and Their Message (9:7-9)

Verse 7 announces that the time of visitation, punishment, and desolation has come; the pay-off day has arrived (see Amos 5:18-20; 8:1-12), and it will be a right dark day (Hosea 10:7-10). Their "great iniquity" and "great hatred" have found them out. Their iniquity was committed against the Lord and their hatred visited upon those who attempted to set them right. Did they not cry out against prophet and man of God? (see Amos 7:10-13). "The prophet is a fool, the man of the spirit is mad," they shouted. The Hebrew word for "fool" used here occurs about twenty-seven times in the Bible and describes the one who is obstinately stupid; in Proverbs it carries with it the idea of licentiousness. Could it be that Hosea was subtly denounced as sharing somehow in the illicit activities of his wife? The root meaning of "mad" is "to rage" and sometimes "lament." Possibly a double meaning is implied here—the prophet rages like a mad dog, he is always uttering lamentations on the condition of the nation. "The man of the spirit" was the truly inspired prophet of God, but beneath the terminology may also lie a feeling of contempt. The Hebrew word for "spirit" also means "wind," and Jeremiah later speaks of the sentiment prevalent in his day to the effect that the prophets were windbags (Jer. 5:13).

Despite the popular attitude, the prophets were true watchmen whose duty it was to warn the people of danger (vs. 8). That is exactly what Hosea was about. The phrase, "the people of my God," reflects Hosea's longing that they might fulfill the Covenantal requirements to remain the people of God. And yet, instead of gratitude for his work and obedience to the word of God which he delivered, there was laid for the prophet a snare wherever he went. There was attempt after attempt to trap him, and possibly get rid of him. Even at the shrine of worship where there should have been a recognition of the truth he preached and the Covenant he shared with them, hatred was his lot. The reason was a deep-seated corruption as determined "as in the days of Gibeah" (vs. 9; see discussion of 10:9). The only response of the prophet was a reiteration of the Lord's judgment.

Baal-peor and Its Consequences (9:10-14)

In this section the contrast between the *then* and the *now* is sharply drawn. Israel's earlier relationship with the Lord is bound up with his love for her and the impression she made upon him by her response to his offer of salvation (deliverance from Egypt) and obedience to his will (instruction). The Lord looked upon these people with the same delight that stirs the heart of a weary and hungry traveler when he comes upon a vine loaded with grapes in a desert oasis or that moves the husbandman to rejoice when he finds the first ripe fig on the tree in the first season of its bearing (9:10). In other words, Israel at first was joy to the heart of the Lord. But she came to Baal-peor (Num. 25:1-5). Baal-peor here stands for the defection which manifested itself as early as the wilderness days and which continued until now. It stood for apostasy and harlotry into which the people fell in Moab. Their acts led to disaster then and they will do so again. They dedicated themselves to "shame" (vs. 10, margin), which is merely a substitute term for "Baal." Thus they became an abomination, "detestable like the thing they loved."

The end result of the pursuit of such abominable conduct will be extinction, loss of country, home, and family (vs. 11). The glory of every Israelite was his family, and that glory will fly away like the bird. The most horrible thing that could befall Israel would be "no birth, no pregnancy, no conception." Israel owed her existence to the Lord and without faith in him and faithfulness to his Covenant she will cease to be, and no matter how many children may be born in her families she will be bereft of them. On the other hand, mere progeny will not guarantee continued existence; only the presence of God can do that (vs. 12). Something of the prophet's feeling on this point appears in his exclamation: "Woe to them when I depart from them!"

The Hebrew text of verse 13 is altogether meaningless as it stands; the Greek version, which the Revised Standard Version follows, is a prophecy of exile and describes a vision in which Ephraim's coming devastation and deportation are threatened. Ephraim will become a prey to the invader and by his guilt will lead his own sons to slaughter at the hands of the enemy.

Verse 14 is an intercession of the prophet for mercy. Slaughter and exile are inevitable because there is no disposition on the part of the people to repent. This is one of the most hopeless passages in Hosea. Most of his prophecy breathes the spirit of hope that some chastisement will bring the nation to its senses and will thus provide the necessary impetus to repent. But there comes a time when the only thing left is drastic surgery. That time had now arrived, the prophet felt, and circumstances would have to run their relentless course. Hence this prayer: "Give them, O LORD—what wilt thou give?" There is no doubt as to what is about to transpire for the nation as a whole. But what about the little ones who were not guilty with their elders? The prayer for miscarrying wombs and dry breasts has a twofold significance—to prevent the birth of innocent children who would be caught in the dreadful events attendant upon foreign invasion (see Lam. 2:11; Matt. 24:19) and to thwart the fertility consequent upon sexual license associated with the practices of their apostate religion. The consequences of Baal-peor will be as disastrous now as they were in the days of Moses.

The Sin of Gilgal (9:15-17)

Here another historical episode is drawn upon to account for the evil tendencies of Israel. First it was Gibeah (9:9; see 10:9-10), then Baal-peor (9:10-14), and now Gilgal. Gilgal was connected with an early sanctuary and condemned by more than one prophet (Amos 4:4; 5:5; Hosea 4:15; 12:11). According to I Samuel 11:14-15, the first king of Israel, Saul, was anointed king there, which act was thought to be a violation of the Covenant which had recognized God alone as King. From the point of view of later writers, when the Philistine problem was forgotten, that was where Israel's troubles began. In any event, there is where "I began to hate them," says the Lord (vs. 15). The sin of Israel was ingrained, as Jeremiah later observed (Jer. 2:22); it was not something that happened overnight. Because of the great evil of their deeds they will be driven out of God's "house," that is, out of his land. The word for "drive out" is used elsewhere for the Lord's banishment of the nations who were in the land of Palestine before Israel came and for his removal of Adam and Eve from Eden (Gen. 3:24), though there is probably no permanency implied here. The last part of the verse appears to refer to the immediate situation, saying in effect, "I can no longer love them since all their princes are rebels."

Using the figure of the vine, the prophet declares the utter bankruptcy of the nation (vss. 16-17). Already she has been smitten and her root is dried up. Under such conditions there can be no fruit for survival, no matter how numerous her children. What a fate for "their beloved children"! Ephraim will be cast off because "they have not hearkened" to the Lord. Again one must recall the reference to Gilgal above, where Israel is represented as taking national direction into her own hands, a veritable rejection of God whose leadership was spurned and whose law was repudiated. Such a state of mind was not conducive to national stability and its issue could lead only to the land of "Nod," or the land of wandering (see Gen. 4:14).

Shame, the Issue of Idolatry (10:1-8)

This section is composed of a series of short sayings dealing with altars and pillars (vss. 1-2), kingless days (vss. 3-4), and the idol (calf) of Bethel (vss. 5-8). All three matters have to do with apostasy, its prevalence and effects.

The figure of the vine as a national symbol occurs quite frequently in the literature of Israel (Isa. 5:1-7; 32:12; Jer. 2:21; Ezek. 17; Joel 1:7). There are several direct and indirect references to it in Hosea, but here is a deliberate comparison. "Israel is a luxuriant vine," whose fruit ripens regularly as an indication of the prosperity enjoyed during the reign of Jeroboam II. The blessings of the nation are compared to the fruitfulness of the vine. But what did she do with those blessings? When her fruit was abundant, to celebrate the productivity of the land she multiplied altars which became "altars for sinning" (see 8:11); when the land prospered she erected pillars, apparently as symbols of the fertility cult. Prosperity thus did strange things to Israel; instead of making her aware of the presence of the Lord, it drew her closer to the fertility religion. What people did with their prosperity was indicative of the direction of their heart. It was divided, as the Hebrew of verse 2 has it; it was possessed of a double standard of loyalty, so that the people worshiped the Lord with their lips while their lives were altogether out of line with their profession (see Isa. 29:13; Mark 7:6). But judgment is at hand; the Lord will cut to pieces their cult objects, both altars and pillars, because they are the source and center of the perpetuation of sin.

The historical reference of verses 3-4 is uncertain, but it probably involves the instability of Israel attendant upon the death of Jeroboam II (see on 7:1-7), possibly after one of the conspiracies when there really was no king. What did it matter now? Matters had progressed to such an extent that no king could save them. If by "king" the Lord himself is meant, he too could do nothing because of their defection. Verse 4, however, seems to indicate that an earthly king is the subject of the prophet's pronouncement. For they speak meaningless words of allegiance to the Lord and make agreements with which he had nothing to do. The result is that judgment sprouts like poisonous weeds. Such judgment is as damaging to Covenantal relationship as a poisonous weed to the one who eats it.

"The inhabitants of Samaria tremble for the calf of Beth-aven" in the face of impending catastrophe (10:5; see the discussion of 8:5). The symbol, which by this time had come to be the real thing, had no power to deliver them and so the people feared for the safety of "the calf." That is but a slightly veiled feeling of contempt for the "god" of the nation (see Isa. 44 for another statement on the powerlessness of idols). On its behalf "its people" perform mourning rites, as do its eunuch priests.

There could have been nothing quite so humiliating to a people as to have the "god" in whom they trusted and whom they worshiped carried away captive. That will now be the case in Israel; its shrine will be yielded to "the great king" as tribute (vs. 6). Thus the "god" to which Israel bore its gifts and offerings will itself become a gift to a greater and more powerful "god," the king of Assyria. Disgust will take hold of the people for their folly and they will become the laughingstock of the nations round about. Samaria's king is as impotent as the idol he and his people serve (vs. 7). He is like a chip floating away on the surface of the water. Instead of being the representative of the Lord and his people, he is but a shadow and has no endurance before the enemy. His power and stability have been nullified by reliance upon and practice of a religion which is sheer idolatry.

"The high places of Aven" (probably Beth-aven or Bethel) are headed for destruction because they are "the sin of Israel" (vs. 8). The local high places, the scene not only of illegitimate worship but of actual licentiousness and debauchery, cannot stand before the wrath of the mighty God of Israel, the Lord. The place where they once stood and where multitudes gathered for celebrations will be covered with thorns and thistles, a fulfillment of the very curse which fell upon the earth when Adam and Eve were thrust from Eden (Gen. 3:18, 24). So horrible will be the desolation and suffering that the people will cry to mountains and hills to hide them or fall upon them. The Day of the Lord will be a day of judgment (see Amos 5:18-20; Isa. 2:19, 21). It is significant that our Lord uses these words to describe the horrors of the Final Judgment (Luke 23: 30).

The Sin of Gibeah (10:9-10)

Reference to Gibeah occurs also in 9:9 (see 5:8), but neither there nor in 10:9 is the precise connection unquestionably certain. A possible connection is with the Gibeah of Judges 19 and 20 where the Levite and his concubine were so shamefully mishandled, and where such violent punitive measures were taken against its inhabitants by the men of Israel. Then there is the Gibeah of Saul (I Sam. 10:26; 11:4), which stands for the sin of the kingdom (see above on 9:15-17). It may be, indeed, that both historical events are within the thinking of the prophet. It appears, however, that in 10:9 the sin of the kingdom is uppermost in the mind of Hosea, because there is a definite play on the word "Gibeah," which is connected with the principle of continuity and with war which shall overtake the people there. On the other hand, it could equally well apply to the lesson of Judges where a campaign of extermination follows the sin of the men of Gibeah. The "double iniquity" referred to in verse 10 certainly points to either "two Gibeahs" or "two sins" stemming from the same source. In the last analysis the meaning would be the same. The kingdom was conceived and born in sin and it could bring forth nothing but sin. The sin of Gibeah can result only in punishment—war will "overtake them in Gibeah." Both the kingdom which led to human pride and self-sufficiency and the sin of the fertility cult with all its extravagances will end in destruction. The Lord will discipline "the wayward" through the "nations" who will assemble against them because of "their double iniquity."

The Inevitable Result of Sin (10:11-15)

In this section attention is first directed to the good old days of the wilderness. In the wilderness Israel was amenable to the guidance and direction of the Lord; she "loved to thresh" (vs. 11); that is, the task to which she was set was delightful and not burdensome. The treading out of the grain was a comparatively easy task, offering all the grain the ox wanted to eat and involving no yoke. So it was with Israel in the wilderness; she was fed by the manna of God without the heavy task of preparing the soil (Deut. 8:4, 16). In the days to come, however, things will be different, for Ephraim must put on the yoke, "Judah must plow" and "Jacob must harrow for himself." The hard lot of exile will be quite a contrast to the blessings so thoughtlessly enjoyed under the provident care of God.

Similar terminology is effectively employed in the prophet's appeal to his compatriots in verse 12. The figure of sowing and reaping is applied to the religious life of the nation. In the land of promise they were to sow righteousness for a harvest of steadfast love, to break up the fallow ground of opportunity because the time for such work was at hand. The response (harvest) was assured, for the Lord was ready to rain salvation upon them. Thus under striking agricultural symbolism is presented one of the most vital truths of our faith—the law of spiritual returns. Those who seek find. The Covenant offered by God comes to full fruition when men seek to obey its terms and apply them in every aspect of their lives. To put it another way, "Whatever a man sows, that he will also reap" (Gal. 6:7).

Whether the exhortation in verse 12 is regarded as made to the fathers only or whether there is present in it an appeal of the prophet to the Israel of his day, its rejection is evident. They have cultivated wickedness and harvested the resultant injustices and consumed the fruit of deception (vs. 13). That was the exact opposite of what should have been the case. Furthermore, the whole religious complex which developed in Israel stressed self-dependence. Fertility rites were always magically applied to force the hand of God, to compel him to give good crops; ritualism was likewise an attempt to coerce the Deity through formal ceremony. An extension of the same principle is found in the treaties and alliances made with foreign powers for protection.

Israel's faith in the pagan tools of war will end in disaster; the very things in which she trusted will of necessity be turned against her (vs. 14). The reference to the battle of Beth-arbel in which Shalman wrought such terrible destruction is totally obscure. We do not know whether Shalman was an Assyrian king or the Shalamann of Moab mentioned in an inscription of Tiglath-pileser III, nor do we know which Beth-arbel is meant. At any rate the event appears to have been fresh in the mind of people and prophet and was used to illustrate what happens to nations who trust in themselves. In verse 15 the application is made to the house of Israel. What happened at Beth-arbel is exactly what will happen in Israel because of her "great wickedness."

On the Fatherly Love of God (11:1-11)

The eleventh chapter of Hosea is, in some respects, one of the greatest chapters in the Bible. It describes, as far as human language can, the attitude and character of God, together with his dealings with his people. Nowhere else is the depth of God's love so sympathetically portrayed. The conception here probably grew out of the prophet's own experience with Gomer and her children.

Israel's Response to God's Love (11:1-2)

Hosea, as most of the other prophets, draws upon past experience, upon historical episodes and events, to drive home the lessons and principles he has in mind for his associates. In harmony with the family ideal, around which most of his preaching revolves, he recalls the youth of Israel, when it was a lad, at the time of the call in Egypt and the wilderness years (11:1). The call came because of the Lord's great love for Israel. Here the regular term for human love is used, as indeed it is throughout the book. It is interesting to observe that the root of the word for "love" employed here occurs nineteen times in Hosea, twice in Amos and Micah, and only once in Isaiah 1-39; it occurs nine times in the rest of Isaiah. As over against the usage of that term for "love," the word for "steadfast love" or "covenant love" occurs only six times in Hosea, three in Micah, once in Isaiah 1-39, and seven times in the remainder of Isaiah; it does not occur at all in Amos. The frequency of occurrences of the word for human love in Hosea (sometimes referred to as "election love" when it relates to the relationship between the Lord and Israel) indicates the source of the sentiment behind the word and the infinite tenderness with which it is charged. Just as Hosea loved his wife and his family with the utmost affection, so the Lord loved Israel as a child. That love led to his call or, better, invitation to Israel to become his adopted son, to be the recipient of his blessings and to enjoy the bounties of his care forever.

One of the fundamental qualities of love as demonstrated by the experience of Hosea is persistence. Something of that notion is reflected in verse 2. "The more I called them" is a telling expression of God's perseverance and the love that will not let his people go. "The more they went from me," on the other hand, tells the story of the nation's apostasy. The parable of our Lord in Luke 20:9-16 is very much to the point.

Early Blessings from the Lord (11:3-4)

How did Israel arrive at the place it now occupied? In an unforgettable figure taken from family life, the prophet points out that it was the Lord who had taught Ephraim to walk; that is, he set him on his feet as a people, as a nation. He it was who took them up in his mighty arms and bore them along (vs. 3). In other words, he had performed the function of father to the people with all the love and care characteristic of the father-child relationship. And yet they did not know that he had healed them (a reflection of the plagues of Egypt from which the Israelites were preserved; see Exod. 15:26). Israel failed to recognize and respond to the fatherly love of God.

From Israel's lack of response, the prophet turns once more to the attitude of the Lord which he has learned to understand, so far as human experience can reflect the spirit of the Lord, through his own feeling for his wife and children. The Lord, throughout history, had carried them along with "compassion" (vs. 4); he did not drag them down the road of life with the hooks of the cruel conqueror (see II Kings 19:28; Isa. 37:29). Instead of the rough, hard cords and bands used to harness oxen, he led them with humane cords and bands of love. The "bands" were used to hold down the yoke on the necks of the oxen. This does not mean that Israel was unharnessed; it means simply, as Jesus said about his yoke (Matt. 11:30), that it was well-fitting, which made the load seem light. The yoke of "Covenant love" was so well-fitting, because of the way the Lord had made it, that it appeared as the easing of "the yoke on their jaws." Or the reference may be to the loosening of the cords that held down the yoke, so that the oxen could eat without choking. In that case, Israel's yoke was not only so loosened that she could eat but the Lord even "bent down to them and fed them" as the considerate plowman fed his oxen. In any event, the verse points to the tenderness of Israel's treatment at the hands of the Lord.

The Reward of Stubbornness (11:5-7)

Because the kindness and consideration of the Lord were thwarted by Israel's stubbornness, it will be necessary for her to relearn the old lessons of hardship, of slavery, of the yoke of Egypt. But this time Assyria will be her Egypt (11:5; see 10:6; Isa. 7:18; 8:4, 7). The one whom they expected as their savior will place a yoke upon their neck, for "Assyria shall be their king." In place of the well-fitting yoke of the Lord will come the raging sword which will destroy them and bring them into subjection to the king of Assyria (vs. 6). Their cities will be ravished, their gates of protection broken down, and their fortified places overthrown. So determined are the people on following their own way that nothing can save them from the yoke which they are about to impose upon themselves (vs. 7).

God's Redeeming Love (11:8-11)

In verses 8-11 the divine pathos finds expression in unparalleled form. The depth of the divine love is nowhere else stated so forcefully and so meaningfully, unless it be in John 3:16. That love is acted out, to be sure, on the Cross, but here the heart of the Eternal is bared in a way which every father and mother can understand. God had brought Israel up as a parent nurtures, protects, provides for, and instructs a child. That child, Israel, had cut the apron strings of the parental relationship and had gone on its own. Baal had taken the place of the Lord and his ways were being followed to the lasting hurt of the Lord's wayward child. But despite the child's waywardness, the Lord will not surrender him; he will persist in the attempt to save him even though the situation looks hopeless. The cry in verse 8, "How can I give you up, O Ephraim! How can I hand you over, O Israel!" expresses the undying love of a parent for his child; no matter what betide, he will never abandon the child. The child may be ever so rude and unresponsive, but the father will never cease loving him. God is like that—bearing and forbearing with us his sinful children. That is the love that will never let Israel go. He cannot do to Israel as he had done with Admah and Zeboiim which belonged to the group of cities of the plain with Sodom and Gomorrah (see Gen. 14:2, 8; 19:24-29; Deut. 29:23), all of which were utterly destroyed because of their very great wickedness. Here, therefore, we have the view that is frequently expressed elewhere: that Israel will not be destroyed root and branch; a remnant will remain, a stump, a shoot from which a new growth will issue. The warmth of God's love is further described in human terms understood by all who have been in Hosea's or a father's place. "My heart recoils within me" expresses the inner conflict between justice and love which, according to the Bible, forever haunts the divine mind. But the latter always wins, for his "compassion grows warm and tender." And in the Cross, God himself pays the penalty for man's sin and satisfies his own justice. Certainly Hosea here has laid hold of a principle of love and compassion whose full import was not made plain until Jesus on his cross exclaimed, "Father, forgive them; for they know not what they do" (Luke 23:34).

Because of his great love, therefore, the Lord will not execute his "fierce anger" nor "again destroy Ephraim," for he is "God and not man, the Holy One in your midst" (vs. 9). The usual attitude of man would have been to wash his hands of the disobedient and ungrateful people. As a matter of fact the usual response of a man toward a wayward wife, too, would have been to seek divorce. But Hosea did not act in that way; he sought his wife and never gave up loving her. Such was the attitude of God toward his people. God does not carry out his judgment upon Ephraim although Ephraim judges himself by refusing to hearken to the appeal of God's men, and so rushes headlong over the precipice to Assyria—to destruction. God moves toward Israel with forgiving love and grace, but Israel chooses to reject both, and in so doing chooses exile.

Verses 10-11 doubtless refer to the recall from exile, the new desert experience into which they thrust themselves (see 2:14-15). After a period of slavery, they will come trembling from all places at the call of the Lord, who will restore "them to their homes." They will be as swift to respond as birds to a call, as ready to listen as they once were quick to disobey and run away from the Lord. Chapter 11 is very closely related to chapter 2 and cannot be understood without constant reference thereto. There Hosea is represented as leading his wife to the wilderness where he can speak reasonably and tenderly to her, persuade her to return, and give her the blessings of family life which her lovers had promised but could not produce. It must not be forgotten that both there and here the family situation and Israel's defection are interwoven. Again, it should be observed that God's love would have spared Israel but Israel would not be spared; but in the desperation of exile a new opportunity would present itself. That is what the prophet hoped for.

On the History of Israel's Sinfulness (11:12—13:16)

The Vision of Jacob (11:12—12:6)

The first part of verse 12 is clear. It speaks of Ephraim's falsehood and deceit with reference to the Lord. The house of Israel is charged with deliberate deception of the Lord in its religious practices. The meaning appears to be that what was called the worship of the Lord was so only in name, and there was a studied attempt to conceal its real nature and purpose from him (see Matt. 7:21). The second part of the verse is not intelligible as it stands in the Hebrew. In the Revised Standard Version it is a comment on the situation in Judah. If it is from Hosea it must belong to the period of King Hezekiah of Judah, under whom an important reformation took place (II Kings 18:4-6) and to which it may refer.

Then the prophet returns to the main theme—deception and falsehood. He has just taken the people to task for their treachery to the Lord. Now he directs his attention to the effect their irreligion is having upon themselves. Ephraim, he says, is shepherding the wind and chasing the east wind "all day long" (12:1; see 8:7); in so doing falsehood and violence are being multiplied and there is no solution to the tantalizing problems afflicting the nation. What Hosea means by the figures he has just used is explained in the concluding part of verse 1. They have entered into a treaty with Assyria and have taken oil to Egypt. Rather than seeking the Lord and practicing the Covenant they are playing the game of international politics and perhaps intrigue.

The language of verse 2 is technical. As in 4:1, Hosea speaks of the Lord's legal case against Israel (which ought to be understood here for "Judah," the latter name being substituted when the prophecy was applied to Judah at a later period). The indictment is regarded as sufficiently proved, so that the sentence is at once pronounced. The sentence is punishment for the nation's "ways" and "deeds." These are customary terms for behavior, either good or bad. Here, of course, they stand for the evil practices so frequently described by the prophet (4:9; 7:2; 9:15; see Matt. 23). Note that judgment is based on acts, the outgrowth of faith or the outworking of rejection of the Covenant faith.

Verse 3 is a lesson drawn from a play on the name of Jacob. Jacob is said to have received his name from the fact that he took his brother Esau by the heel at birth (Gen. 25:26); here that act is set back to the womb, though it signifies nothing more than what is involved in the Genesis account. Jacob means "heel gripper," which in the context must be regarded as referring to the deceptive deeds of the patriarch in his dealings with Esau. But, according to Genesis 32:28, Jacob's name was later changed to Israel, here interpreted to mean perseverance with God.

Hosea views Jacob as a symbol of Israel as it is in his day, deceptive, full of guile, and contentious with God. And just as Jacob, their ancestor, had to face the God who had met him at Bethel, and struggle with him, so God is now speaking to Israel; Israel is at the crossroads, so to speak, and must contend with him. This is the same God that Jacob met—"the LORD the God of hosts, the LORD is his name" (vs. 5). "The LORD of hosts" is a common designation for God in the Old Testament and does not mean simply the general of Israel's armies or of the armies of heaven, though that may have been a part of the original meaning. For the prophets and psalmists it had a much deeper and wider connotation. It included such aspects as the power of God, the rule of God, the leadership of God, and especially the universality of God. That was the nature of the Deity with whom Israel had to deal, and he was as demanding now as in the days of Jacob.

Hence the prophet urged his people to return to God as Jacob did after his spree of deception and guile. They are implored to repent and return to their God (vs. 6; the word "return" has both meanings). That will involve more than confession of guilt, the tossing of a pinch of incense, or even the offering of a costly sacrifice. It will demand a vital change of heart, plus amends for the wrong done, as Jacob found. It demands, further, the maintenance of love and justice with respect to both God and man. "Hold fast" is the same term used in the Hebrew of Deuteronomy 5:12 with reference to "keeping" the Sabbath day holy. It means to guard, observe, keep, and maintain what is enjoined. Observe that both words, "love" and "justice," are Covenantal terms. Perseverance in the Covenant is emphasized by the third element of the verse—"wait continually for your God."

Ephraim and the Lord (12:7-10)

Further characteristics of Israel are drawn upon to drive home the lesson of the Lord's treatment of Ephraim. "Trader" (vs. 7) is a free rendering of the Hebrew word "Canaan" or "Canaanite" and emphasizes the mercantile interests of Israel in the land from the days of Solomon, the greatest merchant prince of antiquity. Israel's activities are likened to the shady dealings of crooked merchants. "False balances" and the will "to oppress" go together; both are severely condemned by prophets and wise men. Again and again a righteous or just weight is stressed as one of the requirements of Covenantal loyalty (Lev. 19:36; Deut.

5:13, 15; Prov. 16:11). The merchant was also the banker, and
cheating in weight was likely to go hand in hand with sharp
money deals and questionable lending policies under which foreclosure could be executed legally but without consideration of
covenantal love and mercy (see Isa. 5:8; Micah 2:2, 4). The result of such practices was riches and wealth, at least for some.
Israel lay astride the caravan routes and took advantage of tolls
which were collected from other merchants of the day. But,
asked the prophet, was it worth it? Certainly all the vaunted
wealth of Israel thus acquired could not "offset the guilt he has
incurred" (vs. 8).

The statement "I am the LORD your God from the land of
Egypt" reflects knowledge of the basis for the Covenant of Sinai
as shown by the introduction to the Ten Commandments in both
Exodus 20 and Deuteronomy 5. The real source of Israel's
wealth and power lies in the Covenant, and not in her self-aggrandizement and improper dealings. To restore the Covenant
relationship is the purpose of the coming exile (see 2:14).

The true Covenant loyalty should have prevailed in Israel
from the beginning until the present, for God had spoken
through prophetic word and vision and parable (vs. 10). The history of the nation testifies to the accuracy of this observation;
think, for example, of Ahijah of Shiloh (I Kings 11, 12, 14, 15),
Micaiah ben Imlah (I Kings 22), Elijah and Elisha (I Kings 17
–II Kings 13). The people had the law of Moses, the instruction
of pious priests, and the direct guidance of the prophets, and
hence should not have been ignorant of God's Covenant or of
the real source of the blessings which they attributed to their
own ingenuity or to Baal.

Gilead and Gilgal (12:11)

For "Gilead" see comments on 6:8 and for "Gilgal" 4:15;
9:15. The references here are somewhat obscure but what the
prophet says about them is rather clear. The iniquity of Gilead
has not come about through the Lord, for it comes to "nought"
(vs. 11). The term "iniquity" here probably refers to some specific illicit act or image (I Sam. 15:23) which had something to
do with Gilead. Sacrifice of bulls at Gilgal, too, has a specific object in view which now escapes us. The whole verse stresses religious practices which were aimed at service of the Lord but which
were actually deceptive devices misleading the people them-

selves. When the invader strikes they will prove useless to prevent destruction and exile. In place of well-wrought altars frequented by worshipers there will be stone heaps in a plowed field, a hindrance to the farmer rather than a help.

God's Prophets and Israel's Response (12:12-14)

The prophecy in verses 12-14 is apparently based on the history of Jacob in "the land of Aram" (Gen. 29-31), which in itself seems to have little to do with the conclusion drawn by the speaker. The connecting idea is "keep" or "preserve." Jacob is represented here, in line with the tradition, as keeping Laban's flocks for his wives. Jacob loyally served Laban for Leah and Rachel; he took excellent care of the family possessions, and they increased and prospered under his shepherding. He did it for the sake of winning a wife (wives). That is the figure under which Hosea conceives the relationship between the Lord and Israel; she is his wife. The fact that not all points of the story of Jacob fit logically into the pattern of thought does not alter the basic truth. As Jacob cared for the sheep for his wives, so the Lord cared for Israel "his wife." He had appointed Moses to lead his people out of Egypt (a thought to which Hosea loved to turn again and again) and direct them to Sinai and the land of promise (vs. 13). After they were in the land he continued to provide and care for them. The same Hebrew word is rendered "herded" in verse 12 and "preserved" in verse 13, and is the regular term employed for taking care of the flock. What was involved is well described in John 10. But what was the attitude of the ones so lovingly cared for? They did exactly what Jesus said Jerusalem did to the prophets (Matt. 23:34-37). They rejected the hand that fed and led them. It was a case of the sheep deserting the shepherd, the wife the husband, the child the father; and such desertion and actual violent opposition could not go on unnoticed or unrefuted. The Lord will leave "his bloodguilt upon him, and will turn back upon him his reproaches" (vs. 14).

Men Kissing Calves (13:1-3)

What a contrast there was between the *then* and the *now!* Once Ephraim was the leader of the nation. The specific reference is not apparent; it could refer to tribal superiority or to the position of the Northern Kingdom after the disruption of the Solomonic empire when ten tribes withdrew to form a kingdom (I

Kings 12:20), or it could refer to the successes of the northern state under Jehoash (II Kings 14:11-14) and Jeroboam II (II Kings 14:25-27). In earlier times, "When Ephraim spoke, men trembled" (Hosea 13:1), but now matters were altogether different. Why? "He incurred guilt through Baal and died." When the Lord's Covenant was upheld the nation was strong, but when the subversions of Baalism set in, weakness and trouble followed. By this time the death of the true Israel had already taken place. All that was needed now was burial in the far-off land of Assyria.

When the seeds of death were once sown the resultant weeds were hard to control. When Israel once adopted the forms and *ritual* of Canaan the logical and almost inevitable outcome was the *practice* of Canaanism. So they continued to sin, to depart more and more from the true ideal of one God who demands holiness on the part of his devotees (vs. 2). Adoption of the forms of Canaan did not stop with copying of building, altar, and ritual; it led to further embellishments—they made "for themselves molten images, idols skillfully made of their silver." The furniture of Israel's formal worship was ever on the increase, and the simplicity of the desert was forgotten. More and more care was bestowed on the production and design of the material elements of worship, as the expressions "their silver" and "all of them the work of craftsmen" indicate. These elements became objects of worship in themselves rather than avenues for worship of the Lord. The prophet could not understand how his fellows reasoned—"Sacrifice to these, they say," as if they had been commanded to do so. It had become a real and significant part of their lives. "Men kiss calves!" Kissing was a symbol of submission, as may be seen from the Assyrian inscriptions and monuments (see also Ps. 2:12; I Kings 19:18). Behind Hosea's statement is an utter disgust, unmatched elsewhere. Because they had come to reverence what Jeremiah later called "no gods" (Jer. 2:11) they themselves have no substance. Nothing plus nothing equals nothing! In verse 3 the figures of the "morning mist" (see 6:4), the "dew" (6:4), the "chaff" (Job 21:18; Pss. 1:4; 35:5), and "smoke" (Pss. 68:2; 102:3; Isa. 51:6) symbolize the passing, the temporal and evanescent. The Lord is eternal, but what Israel made and worshiped would be swept away.

The Fate of Those Who Forget God (13:4-11)

It will be observed that throughout the prophecy Hosea is the mouthpiece of God, that all the statements are in the first person. God has literally "put on" Hosea (see Judges 6:34; II Chron. 24: 20), who speaks the words of the Lord. So he reaffirms that "I am the LORD your God" (13:4). He has been their God since their deliverance from Egypt, after which they acknowledged him and entered into a solemn Covenant with him. The Lord had been their deliverer, or savior, from Egypt and during the untoward events of the wilderness experience (vss. 4-5). He had loved his people, cared for them, and delivered them from dangers in the land of promise. Only with the living God did they have vital fellowship. The affirmation, "I . . . knew you in the wilderness" (vs. 5), with emphasis on the "I," refers to the events recounted in the Book of Numbers (see also Amos 3:2). "The land of drought" is literally "the land of fever," a word used only here in the Old Testament. It can refer to a hot and dry land, but also probably to the illnesses which struck Israel in the days of wandering (Num. 12:3-15; 14:37-38; 21:6-7; ch. 25). Despite their troubles, brought on by defection of one kind or another, the Lord remained with them, as he had promised.

The Deuteronomist speaks of the Lord's warning that when the people enter the land and enjoy its gifts they must not forget their God who was responsible for these blessings (Deut. 6:10-12; 8:7-20). But that warning went unheeded and when the people were sated with food and the other blessings of the land "their heart was lifted up" (vs. 6), that is, they became haughty, insolent, and proud. In the new land they imagined that it was their observance of the agricultural ritual which brought them food and drink, and so they forgot the Lord.

There is only one step from forgetfulness to judgment. For the unsuspecting, judgment lurks in the most unlikely places (vss. 7-8). The security and peace of the Lord will become the insecurity of the wilderness, where wild beasts wait in every hiding place to pounce upon anyone who comes their way. Wild beasts do not lurk by the wayside unless they are hungry or have been chased. That characteristic accentuates the intense feeling of the Lord toward Israel: he has been aroused like a vicious beast, though we are not to assume that the prophet attributes beastly qualities to him. It is his way of expressing as vividly as possible the concern of the Lord for his people, particularly because they have rejected his way of protective care in exchange for the insecurities of international diplomacy and flagrant immorality. What is meant by the figures employed is that instead of the shepherding provision which Israel has experienced at the hand of her God she will presently have to endure the ruthlessness and heavy hand of the conqueror. He will be as fierce as the robbed bear; he will drag them to the desert (exile) and, like a lion, devour them without mercy. And that was precisely what happened in the captivity of Israel by the Assyrians.

The warning becomes more specific in the following verses. Israel will definitely be destroyed. Evidently Hosea had by this time given up all hope for his people's repentance and consequent deliverance. Hence the blunt assertion, "I will destroy you, O Israel" (vs. 9). The word for "destroy" is used by the writer of Genesis 6:17 and 9:15 with reference to the Flood with its utter and complete destruction. It fits quite well the situation contemplated by Hosea. "Who can help you?" inquires the prophet. The obvious answer is "No one." Certainly the "no gods" are impotent and will be an impediment rather than help on that day. Only the Lord can help, and they have rejected him.

Ironically, the king who was supposed to be Israel's savior, her helper, had become her enemy (vs. 10). The kings are represented as having been appointed because of the wrath of God, inasmuch as the demand of the people constituted a repudiation of the rule of God himself (vs. 11). Even so, however, it was the king's duty to act as the representative of God in all matters pertaining to the welfare of the people and to carry out his will for them. But many of the kings looked to their own interests and cared little about the people or God. That was especially true of the last four kings of Israel. They were usurpers or puppets of foreign powers, whose purposes they served. The characterization of the king which had been given in I Samuel 8:11-18 proved to be only too true in the experience of both kingdoms, but the climax in each came in a final onslaught against them, when the monarchs were worse than useless.

Struggle for Rebirth (13:12-14)

In a very real sense Hosea is a prophet of hope, and he never gives up the cause for Israel. That is because of his very nature; a husband who could not rest until he had made the last possible move to rescue his wayward wife could not conceive of the living God as leaving off the pursuit of his people. To be sure, the sins of the nation could not be passed over lightly; in fact, they were "kept in store" (vs. 12). The figures of speech employed are most revealing. To bind up iniquity means to wrap it up like a document in cloth or papyrus and store it in a place for safekeeping like a treasure. Was there still a possibility of change of heart, or was the prophet dimly aware of something in the distant future?

From the figure of books upon which were kept the records of men's lives, the prophet turns to another equally suggestive of hope—that Israel might have a rebirth (vs. 13). This is the principle taken up in John 3 with such penetrating insight. Obviously this message is somehow related to the earlier assertion of Israel's death to the Lord while she was still alive to Baal (13:1). Israel is thus likened to a child which is undergoing all the pangs of birth but cannot be born. The pains of the nation are evident on every side but still there is no issue—a remarkable description of the historical situation! There is not the strength and vitality to burst forth from the matrix of the situation. The child, without the wisdom (religious strength) to present itself at the mouth of the womb, was destined to perish there, in the womb of the time.

Had the prophet already presented a plea to the Lord on behalf of Israel such as even the much harsher Amos had done? (Amos 7:2-3, 5-6). Whether that is so, or whether there is here a pronouncement of the Lord's determination to save the nation despite its guilt, depends on the translation of verse 14, which is itself dependent upon its last clause—"Compassion is hid from my eyes." If the prophet had argued for mercy for the nation, his argument seems to have been overruled by the Lord. If that is true, then we must follow the Revised Standard Version in lines one and two of the verse, and perhaps put the thought even more strongly—"*Can* I ransom . . . *Can* I redeem?" The question then is: is there still a possibility of deliverance? How can God redeem or ransom a people who refuse to permit him to do so? Lines three and four then become a call for the plagues of death and the pestilences of Sheol to begin their work; for nothing more can be done to save them.

The Result of Samaria's Guilt (13:15-16)

That the preceding section is concerned with the doom of Israel is confirmed by this one, which insists upon the fact that Samaria is about to reap the fruit of her rejection of the Lord in a horrible calamity. The nation is portrayed under the figures of a reed plant, a fountain, and a spring. So sure is the impending judgment that though she should flourish in the midst of reed plants (which may refer to the expectation of support from Egypt), an east wind of the Lord coming from the desert will sweep her away. The dreaded sirocco (southeast wind), which blows across the desert in Palestine at almost any time during the summer, has the effect of lifting the temperature from fifteen to twenty degrees and reducing the humidity some thirty per cent. It affects quite adversely man, beast, and vegetation (see Jonah 4:8; Ps. 103:16). Here, however, the east wind probably has a more specific meaning, referring to Assyria whose invasion cannot be stopped by Egyptian aid. Israel's treasury will be ravaged of "every precious thing," that is, its sacred and secular treasures.

Verse 16 voices the inevitable outcome of the stubborn and rebellious attitude of the nation, here symbolized by Samaria, the capital city of the kingdom. Samaria must accept the responsibility for her acts and decisions. From the prophetic point of view she had "rebelled" against God, and the fate of rebels is a hard one indeed (Num. 16:31-35; Ps. 106:17-18; I Sam. 12:15; Isa. 1:20; 63:10). The warning that "they shall fall by the sword" is best explained by reference to either the invasion of Tiglath-pileser III in 733 B.C. (II Kings 15:29) or that of Shalmaneser V in 724 B.C. (II Kings 17:1-6). The campaign of the former and Sargon II's overthrow of Samaria are recorded in the Assyrian inscriptions. The horrible scene depicted in the latter part of the verse obviously reflects the conditions following the break-through of a siege, particularly after a long and hard one (see Nahum 3:10; II Kings 8:12).

THE OFFER OF SALVATION TO
A PENITENT PEOPLE

Hosea 14:1-9

The last chapter of the Book of Hosea takes the form of a penitential liturgy consisting of the usual three parts: the call to repentance, the penitential prayer, and the reponse of the Lord. Many interpreters have denied the authenticity of the chapter because it appears to be out of line with the predictions of utter and irrevocable doom as set forth, for example, in the preceding chapter. There is, however, no internal or external evidence by which it can be dated with any degree of certainty, and hence we do not know from what period of Hosea's activity it comes. There is no basis for a denial of authorship by Hosea because quite a number of his undisputed oracles either assert outrightly or breathe the spirit of hope. The very fact that a prophet undertook to speak in the name of the Lord is itself an indication of his belief in the possibility of repentance and therefore of hope. And Hosea is above all else a prophet of hope, as may be seen from the first three chapters. He stood in the intimate council of the Lord and so was aware of the attitude of the Lord who before the time of the prophet and after it persisted in his offer to man—finally sending his Son as an earnest of his love.

The Offer of the Lord Through the Prophet (14:1-3)

It is not difficult to understand the final call of the Lord as transmitted through Hosea in view of the deep concern for Israel expressed in chapter 11. The prophetic summons is issued in hope and with all the urgency its author could put into it. Hence he begins with the simple and unqualified demand for repentance, for that is what "return" to the Lord here means (14:1). But before repentance or return to the Lord could take place there would have to be a recognition and confession of sin. Hosea, therefore, declares, without qualification: "You have stumbled because of your iniquity." But Israel can yet be forgiven (restored) if she confesses her wrongdoing and takes up again the Covenantal relationship with the Lord.

For the re-establishment of that relationship they must, as a people, return to the Lord with "words" rather than sacrifices (vs. 2). That can mean one of two things: the ritual approach whereby some kind of formal confession must be made and absolution pronounced, or the offering of *things* ("word" and "thing" are expressed by the same Hebrew term); that is, the offering of deeds—the "fruit that befits repentance" (Matt. 3:8). In the latter case it would signify the sacrifice of the broken and contrite heart (Ps. 51:17) which expresses itself in renewed fellowship with God and the performance of his will. Actually, perhaps, both elements were combined in the mind of the prophet, who thought of the "prayer" offerings of the worshiper, the counterpart of which must always be the surrender of life to the purpose of God. This seems to be the import of the simple ritual which he enjoins—"say to him, 'Take away all iniquity; accept that which is good and we will render the fruit of our lips' " (vs. 2). Elsewhere he speaks of the "fruit of lies" (10:13), which is the opposite of the fruit of the repentant lips. To speak a word was to create something described by that word; hence the declaration of the fruit of the lips means the creation of the word-deed intended by the speaker, which in this instance is repentance with its fruits in life.

But renewal, as has been said above, is dependent upon a recognition that the way they have followed has led them to despair and desolation (vs. 3). International diplomacy (intrigue) cannot save them; Assyria is incapable of doing what she claimed, and the "horses" (of Egypt? see I Kings 10:28) are equally helpless. Does such recognition of the bankruptcy of foreign alliances follow the fall of Samaria, or the beginning of the siege, or one of the several periods antedating those events when both powers proved deceptive?

The other besetting sin of Israel was idolatry, the work of men's hands (vs. 3). The futility of confidence in man-made gods was demonstrated on more than one occasion and now has shown its supreme folly. This, too, the people must see and must confess in all sincerity before the Lord in their penitential service. Israel had really orphaned herself by her deeds; her idols were no gods and her alliances failed her. Hence she must also understand that she is an orphan, an outcast, and can exclaim only, "In thee the orphan finds mercy."

Divine Restoration and Its Consequences (14:4-8)

As might be expected from the form of the confession above and the character of the prophet's faith, the people's entreaty made in repentance draws an eager and welcome response from the Lord. These verses constitute the divine answer to the confession and prayer. As such they represent the profound faith of the writer in the goodness and steadfast love of God. They form the absolution after the confession and are filled with all the redemptive qualities we are led to associate with God. Israel's sin, which was likened to sickness by Hosea (5:13), will be healed (14:4; see Jer. 3:22). "Faithlessness" is apostasy, which adequately describes the attitude and practice of the nation after the time of Jeroboam II. Along with the healing of her sin-sickness, the Lord will offer Israel his love once more as he did when she was a slave in Egypt. (On the meaning of the word for "love" here, see comments on 3:1 and 11:4.) That love is offered voluntarily, and with complete forgetfulness of Israel's apostate state, for the Lord's anger has abated by virtue of the people's repentance.

The blessings that accompany God's forgiving love will be as numerous and satisfying as were those showered upon her in the early days in the wilderness. He will be like "the dew to Israel" (vs. 5), which is here used in the customary sense of a moistening agent in time of drought, much appreciated by the agriculturalist (II Sam. 1:21; I Kings 17:1; Gen. 27:28; Deut. 33:28). The blessing of the Lord will make her "blossom as the lily" (literally "a big flower," perhaps of the iris or tulip family). Her roots will be struck down deep like those of the poplar (a somewhat uncertain word since the Hebrew has "Lebanon"). Israel will be as prolific as the shoots which spring out from the stump of a tree; her beauty and splendor will be like the ubiquitous and proud olive, and her fragrance like Lebanon with its cedars and sweet-smelling plants (vs. 6; see Song of Solomon 4:11). The loveliest of figures are here employed to describe the consequences of Israel's repentance and forgiveness, all of which are due to the forgiving love of the Lord and not to any deserts of nation or people. God's goodness will not only restore her but make her beautiful, fruitful, deep-rooted, and fragrant in the world.

Verse 7 continues a slight variation of the theme by a portrayal of the character of the repentant people from the point of view of the Lord. This new status and quality of the people obtains only when "they shall return." In other words, their petition and the Lord's forgiveness constitute a new relationship between themselves and the Lord, in which they will dwell beneath his "shadow." To dwell in the shadow of the Lord indicated security, protection, and care (see Judges 9:15; Pss. 17:8; 91:1; Isa. 51:16). Under his husbandry they will "flourish as a garden" (see Isa. 58:11; Jer. 31:12). The Hebrew text points to the material prosperity of the people—"They shall grow grain." Also "they shall blossom as the vine," which is prolific in the valleys of Palestine and is a symbol of the nation (Ps. 80:8; Ezek. 17:7; Hosea 10:1). The meaning of "fragrance . . . like the wine of Lebanon" is somewhat uncertain, but doubtless it refers to a particularly fine quality of scented wine produced in the Libanus and at Helbon (Ezek. 27:18). The rich agricultural figures describe vividly and with master strokes the hopes of the prophet for his people when they are restored to fellowship with the Lord.

Forgiven and prosperous Israel will then cease to long after or even think of Baal, upon whom they relied so disastrously in times past. Then they will see who it really is who cares for them, for "It is I who answer and look after you" (vs. 8). The Lord alone, a strong monotheistic conception, is their security, "like an evergreen cypress"—the only biblical passage that compares the Lord to a protective tree. Cypress trees do not bear fruit but are used to provide shade and as windbreaks. Along with protection goes provision: "from me comes your fruit."

The Lesson of the Book (14:9)

Verse 9 is obviously a summary of the lesson of the prophecy of Hosea, attached by a later hand, and is in the form of a piece of proverbial wisdom. It is an exhortation to the prudent reader to "understand these things," to discern and apply the teachings of the book (see Prov. 1:2). He is to be circumspect and enter into the spirit of them so as to enjoy the blessings attendant upon their full observance. To "know them" means to be dominated by them in personal and social experience. The history of the nation as well as that of individuals within the nation clearly demonstrates the rightness of the ways and acts of God. He has shown his steadfast love, the binding nature of his Covenant, and the validity of his grace. The righteous walk in his ways. Those who are rebellious refuse to do so because they do not know him or understand him; their end is like that of disobedient Israel. Transgressors stumble to destruction "in them" or "over them" (see Matt. 21:44, margin).

The teaching of the book centers about the call to repentance and salvation which is extended to Israel through the prophet. That call comes by virtue of the Covenant love of God, which itself is expressive of his character and nature. He is a loving and forgiving God, a fact which is an invitation to repentance and which is powerfully illustrated by our Lord in his parable of the Lost Son (Luke 15:11-32).

THE BOOK OF

JOEL

INTRODUCTION

Authorship and Date

There has never been any serious question that the prophet
Joel was the author of the oracles collected under his name. He
is mentioned only once in the book and once in the New Testament (Acts 2:16). The name means "the LORD is God." That he
was a resident of Judah is almost certain because he speaks fer-
vently about Jerusalem and Judah, in whose fortunes he was apparently involved. He was deeply concerned about the contemporary worship but was probably not himself a priest.

The date of Joel must be determined by evidence within the
book since the superscription does not contain any reference to
a king whose period can be fixed from other sources. The prophecy has been placed anywhere from the ninth to the second century B.C. The chief arguments for an early date are: the position
of the book in the Hebrew Canon of the minor prophets (between Hosea and Amos; the Greek translation has it between
Micah and Obadiah), and the mention of the valley of Jehoshaphat in 3:2 and 12 (Jehoshaphat was a king of Judah in the ninth
century B.C.). But stronger factors point to a later date. Although some students place it just before the Babylonian Exile,
chiefly on the grounds of parallels to the prophecy of Jeremiah,
most interpreters today date it after the Exile. The book makes no
reference to either Assyria or Babylonia, nor is there mention of
the Greeks as a world power; they are put in the same category
with Tyre and Philistia, which points to colonizing and trading activity. That would place our book somewhere between the fall of
Babylon and the coming of Alexander the Great. But there are
perhaps more definite hints. The parceling out of the land (3:2)
points to a time not too far removed from the fall of Jerusalem
in 587 B.C. So does the slave trade mentioned in 3:6, when the
whole region was unsettled and at the mercy of those more powerful groups. The bitterness against the Edomites (3:19) is best

explained as coming at a time shortly after the Jerusalem debacle. The Sabeans who must have been operating at this time (3:8) were no longer in control after the sixth century. The poverty of the people, accentuated by plague and drought, and the unsatisfactory character of the ritual service reflect the situation of Haggai and Zechariah. All these factors appear to place Joel somewhere in the crucial period before the completion of the Second Temple in 516 B.C.

The Purpose of the Book

The purpose of the book is to call nation and people to repentance because the Day of the Lord is near. The writer attempts to encourage his hearers in the face of incalculable hardships and at the same time warn them to take stock of themselves.

The Literary Form of the Book

The major portion of the book is poetic in form, probably more so than appears in the English translation, and as such contains the usual features of parallelism and meter. The poetic oracles abound in figures of speech—the locusts are described as a nation, or an army, or a people; they have teeth like lions and fangs like lionesses; they appear like war horses, and their movement is like that of chariots; they scale walls like soldiers. The prosperity following the plague is like the mountains dripping sweet wine and the hills flowing with milk. The impending judgment is called a ripe harvest, a full wine press, overflowing vats.

There is frequent repetition as well as contrast. An example of the former is found in 1:4, 10-12 and of the latter in 3:19-20. Usually there is an ascending scale of parallels which heighten the effectiveness of a given thought as in 1:14; 2:15-16, 28; 3:18.

The Message of Joel

The Day of the Lord

The central teaching of Joel is that the Day of the Lord is at hand (3:13-14) or that it is rapidly approaching. The locust plague with its accompaniments is a sure sign that the great and terrible Day is near. The prophet uses this concept, already two centuries old in his day (Amos 5:18-20), and applies it to the situation at hand. For the earlier prophets, Amos and Zephaniah, the Day of the Lord was an evil day, sweeping away everything before it, like the Flood in the days of Noah. For Joel it was a day of both judgment and salvation. The constant nearness of the Day as viewed by Joel is also a feature of the New Testament (Matt. 3:2, 7-10; 4:17; Mark 1:14-15). The Day is always near, the harvest ripe, the Kingdom of heaven at hand.

Repentance as Preparation for the Day of the Lord

Because of the nearness of the Day, the prophet calls for repentance (2:12-14). For him the plague is a sure harbinger of the Day and demands immediate action on the part of the whole nation (2:15-16). To meet the situation it is necessary to return to the Lord (repent) sincerely and honestly. For those who thus repent, destruction may be averted and the Day become one of salvation, because the Lord is "gracious and merciful, slow to anger, and abounding in steadfast love" (2:13). This appears to have been also the theme of the preaching of John the Baptist (Matt. 3:7-10), though there the reference is to repentance of the individual rather than to that of the nation.

The Right Kind of Worship

Joel evidently is closely associated with the worship ceremonies of the day and has a profound appreciation of the sacrificial rites. But he is equally aware of the fact that pure worship is meant to be an expression of sincere repentance. That is why he demands a rending of the heart rather than the easy outward rending of garments (2:13). He insists also that genuine humility and fasting (2:12) are essential ingredients of true worship.

The Efficacy of Prayer

Joel does not mention private prayer, apart from 1:19, but he is an exponent of corporate prayer, as indicated in 2:17. The priests were to voice the urgent petitions of the people before the Lord in the solemn assembly. The prophet's declaration of the consequent response of the Lord is a clear witness to his belief in the efficacy of sincere corporate prayer.

Salvation for All Who Call Upon the Name of the Lord

This is perhaps the outstanding religious teaching of Joel (2:32). It is certainly salvation by faith, for without faith in God's power and love one could not call upon the name of the Lord. It is still true that the nation is uppermost in the mind of the prophet, but there may be more in the passage than appears on the surface, for the Hebrew, which reads "everyone who calls upon the name of the Lord," indicates that individual members of the nation are deeply involved.

Judgment

Conversely, judgment is the lot of all who do not repent or who fail to call upon the name of the Lord. God will judge his people. (See the commentary on 3:2 and 12.) But he is righteous and merciful (2:12-14) in the rendering of his judgment.

The Promises of the Lord

Joel may be called the prophet of promise. The Lord promises restoration and renewed prosperity in the wake of repentance, freedom from molestation by enemies, vindication of the people, and the ultimate failure of the guilty.

The promise that has received most emphasis, however, is the one having to do with the gift of God's "spirit" (2:28-32). Here are the seeds of true spiritual worship whose full flowering is now in progress in the Christian experience of the Holy Spirit (see Acts 2).

OUTLINE

COMMENTARY

PLAGUE AND ITS RESULTS
Joel 1:1—2:11

The first section of Joel deals with the problem confronting the people in the form of a locust plague and a severe drought. The combined adversities brought on great calamity and led the prophet to proclaim the impending Day of the Lord.

The Superscription of the Book (1:1)

This is all that we know of the prophet in a formal way. No details of call, situation, or historical relationships are given; only his name and that of his father and the all-important fact that he had an experience with "the word of the LORD." The name means "the LORD is God" and was borne by at least thirteen other persons mentioned in the Bible (see Concordance). There is no specified vision or other credential; it is just the word of the Lord for the time, and it was obviously accepted as such.

The Locust Plague (1:2-7)

The immediate occasion for the word of the Lord which came to Joel was a devastating plague of locusts which ravished the land and brought on a serious famine, so that the people were faced with starvation and death. For the prophet it was a time for self-examination and inventory of the causes underlying this judgment of the Lord.

Appeal to Memory (1:2-3)

The prophecy begins with imperatives—"hear . . . give ear"—which call attention to the word of the Lord, but more directly and challengingly to the event which is actually transpiring before their eyes. The elders and "all inhabitants of the land" are directed to give thought to the calamity that is upon them. Verse 2 stresses the severity of the plague with its accompanying circumstances. Never in the memory of those alive had such a thing been experienced in the land, as indicated by the question which manifestly expects a negative answer. They are to mark well the lesson to be derived from the experience so as to be able to relate it to their children, and the story is to be told and retold in coming generations. Joel thus looks upon this event as comparable to the other great events of Israel's history which were to be passed on from generation to generation, inculcating respect for and faith in the Lord (see Exod. 10:2; Deut. 4:9; 6:7; 11:19; Joshua 4:6-7). The other events, of course, were mighty acts of salvation, whereas this one has to do with a catastrophic event. Yet even so it is to be remembered as a lesson which is to be recalled to the coming generations as a deterrent to sin.

The Locusts (1:4-5)

The devastating results of the locust plague are depicted in the Hebrew with untranslatable vigor and force. The description of the development of the locusts themselves is so vivid and striking that one can visualize the several stages of growth and the damage wrought by each. It is relatively certain that the prophet refers to four stages of locust growth and not four types of locusts. If that assessment of the matter is correct, Joel must have been a keen observer. He here recognizes four phases of growth characterized by certain activity: cutting locust—larva stage; swarming locust —the flying, or full-grown locust; hopping locust—the earliest larva; destroying locust—the full-grown locust before it becomes a flying insect. The detailed description of the locusts, together with parallels in ancient Near Eastern literature, indicates that the prophet was not referring to a foreign army or armies invading the land, but to a real locust plague such as periodically overtakes Palestine.

The outlook was so ominous that Joel demanded an awakening on the part of his complacent compatriots. The "drunkards" were urged to take note because they were naturally the first to lament the shortage of wine. But all the people used wine to some extent and they, too, would come to feel the pinch. Lack of wine, following the destruction of the vineyards, was possibly the first sign of the effect of the plague. Therefore, let those who were the first to experience it "awake . . . and wail."

The Devastation (1:6-7)

Invasion of the land by locusts is compared to the coming of a nation because of their multitude. They are described as "powerful and without number." The two terms are really synonymous, for "powerful" here means strong by virtue of number (see Exod. 1:9; Isa. 60:22; Micah 4:7; Dan. 11:25). In 1889 a locust flight extending over 2000 miles passed over the Red Sea; a rough calculation indicated that it numbered 24,420 billions of insects. The havoc that could be wrought by such an army of locusts is incalculable. Not only were the locusts of Joel numerous and powerful but they were armed with weapons of destruction. Their saw-like teeth were like those of an African lion, their "fangs," that is, jawteeth, were like those of the lioness (see also Rev. 9:8). They laid waste vineyard and fig grove; they "stripped off their bark . . . their branches are made white"—a telling indication of their onslaught. Pictures taken after a locust plague in 1915 show branches of trees completely devoid of bark and glisteningly white in the heat of the sun. The poetic metaphor takes account of the two chief fruit-producing trees of the land, the basic sources of sustenance for the people (see Micah 4:4). The emphasis upon *my* land, *my* vines, and *my* fig trees points up the concern of the Lord for his land and its provisions for his people. The vine is elsewhere symbolic of the nation and so may contain a subtle allusion to the fate of the people as a consequence of the plague. In any case, the plague wrought calamity for land and people.

The Effect of the Plague (1:8-20)

The Lament of the People (1:8-12)

The primary effect of the plague is the lack of produce of the land. The land is addressed as a virgin (see Amos 5:2) whom the prophet calls to mourn the catastrophe as a maiden who laments for the bridegroom. Here is a potent figure of the Lord as the bridegroom and the land as the maiden (virgin), the relationship being disrupted by the plague. Putting on sackcloth was common practice in time of mourning (Amos 8:10). The appearance of the land after the plague was indeed distressing; it was in a state of mourning. But what disturbed the prophet was the cessation of sacrifice because there was nothing to sacrifice. "The cereal offering and the drink offering are cut off" (vs. 9), because the locusts had destroyed the grain and the vine. That meant a breaking off of fellowship with the Lord. The reference to offerings here is doubtless to the daily oblations offered

morning and evening at the Temple in accordance with Exodus
29:38-42 and Numbers 28:3-8. Without those offerings the people felt loss of contact with the Lord, and the priests, who understood their significance, mourned.

Verse 10 describes the condition of the land in a striking way.
Field and land are personifications, as they are frequently in
the Old Testament (see Isa. 33:9; Jer. 12:4, 11). In times of
crop failure the land was said to mourn, in times of abundance
to rejoice and sing (Ps. 65:12-13). Since the locust plague came
in a period of drought, it would not take long for all vegetation
to dry up and vanish, with resultant famine in home and shrine.
The mourning of the land would be expected to produce a corresponding effect on farmer and vinedresser. That is why the
prophet addresses them as he does, calling upon them to show
their concern for the crops ruined by drought and plague. Wheat
and barley harvests were lost, vine and fig, pomegranate, palm,
and apple trees were stripped. The last part of verse 12 is really
not co-ordinate with the preceding but is an ejaculation of the
poet reasserting the sentiment of the people, saying in effect,
"Verily, gladness has withered away from the sons of men."

The Call for Solemn Prayer (1:13-14)

As the land, farmers, and vinekeepers have been summoned
to mourning, the priests are now called upon to join in lamentation because their rites are also suffering. The situation demands
special recognition on their part because they are the ministers
of the Lord and are charged with the responsibility of keeping
the people in fellowship with him. They occupy the position of
representatives of the Lord before the people and vice versa, and
thus are charged to act for the people. Land and occupant and
priest must combine to humble themselves before the Lord, and
at the same time to exhibit before him their fasts and prayers. In
times of adversity that was the usual procedure—humility, fasting, and prayer on the part of all concerned. As the people
mourn elsewhere, so the priests are to mourn at the shrine, going
in and passing the night in sackcloth (see II Sam. 12:16). They
are to do this as representatives of the people, because they have
no produce to provide for the regular offerings which "are withheld from the house of your God." Not only so, but they are
charged to provide further for "a fast" and "a solemn assembly,"
that is, to prepare a public fast and assembly. To it were to be

summoned "the elders and all the inhabitants of the land." The elders were the officials of the land. The phrase "all the inhabitants of the land" points to the small community resident in and around Jerusalem after the return from exile. The whole community was thus to come together to confess before the Lord, implore his forgiveness, and plead for restoration and a renewal of their relationship with him. That is the meaning of "cry to the LORD," which signifies intercession for themselves.

The Reason for the Assembly (1:15-18)

According to the prophets, such catastrophic events were the harbingers of the Day of the Lord (see Amos 4:6-12), which would prove disastrous unless the people repented. Hence the catastrophes were really God's call to repentance. The locust plague and drought are a sign that the Day is at hand. Like Amos (Amos 5:18-20), Joel thinks of it as a day of trial by fire, as destruction, not as a day of salvation for Judah and destruction only for the enemy. To reinforce his conception of the seriousness of the situation and his belief in the proximity of judgment, he points to the fact that food has been cut off from the land and the usual joy and happiness attendant upon worship have turned into sadness and mourning. Nature appears to have conspired with the locusts so that the very soil has become impervious; the seed shrivels and dries up, the storehouses and granaries are empty, and the cattle groan and wander about perplexed over the barren pasture lands. These things are taking place "before our eyes," as if to say that the lesson is evident and plain.

The Prayer (1:19-20)

In conjunction with the others whom he has called upon to gather in solemn assembly before the Lord, Joel offers his own prayer of intercession on behalf of the people and in their name. In his prayer he recites existent conditions. The fires of drought and plague have consumed the places where cattle and sheep grazed, something like our prairies. Vivid and striking is the assertion that "Even the wild beasts cry to thee" (vs. 20). The Hebrew for "cry" occurs only here and in Psalm 42:2. It means literally "to incline towards with longing"; the wild animals look up to the Lord with desirous eyes because their pastures are gone and the streams are dried up. For the effect of drought on the wild animals see Jeremiah 14:5-6. Thus the prayer of the prophet calls attention to the suffering of man and beast because of the ravages of the plague, and humbly implores the Lord for forgiveness and mercy. But it also looks forward to even more dire possibilities of judgment which he hopes may be averted by repentance and a return to the Lord.

The Signs of the Day of the Lord (2:1-11)

The Impending Day of the Lord (2:1)

Once again Joel proclaims the nearness of the Day of the Lord by summoning the priests to sound the alarm. The blowing of the horn (trumpet) was the common sign of warning, alerting a city to impending danger (Hosea 5:8; Jer. 6:1; I Cor. 14:8). The plague was obviously the token of worse things yet to come and warranted the sounding of the danger signal. But the signal was to be given from the "holy mountain," that is, from Zion, to call the people to fast and repent. The urgency of the call is indicated by the fact that the people are to respond by trembling, to be genuinely aroused to the situation.

The Plague as the Forerunner of the Day of the Lord (2:2-11)

This is a reiteration, in more elaborate terms, of the appearance of the locust plague as a sign of the approaching Day of the Lord. Quoting from Zephaniah 1:15, Joel describes it as "a day of darkness and gloom, a day of clouds and thick darkness!" (2:2). Amos (5:18) had declared it to be a day of darkness and not light, a day of calamity and desolation. Darkness was a synonym for evil, and since the Day of the Lord was considered by the prophets to bring adversity it was a gloomy, beclouded day. The arriving locusts spread darkness over the land (see Exod. 10:15), as many modern observers of the phenomenon have testified. Like a mighty host they moved across the land, rank after rank, destroying everything in their path. The awesomeness of their appearance, their numbers, and their ravages were unparalleled in history, and the prophet predicts that they will not be paralleled in the future. That is manifestly a reference to the locusts as forerunners or instruments of judgment (see Rev. 9:2-3). The same is probably true of the reference to fire in verse 3. The concept is derived, in part at least, from the desolation pre-

ceding and following the locust plague when the land was first
scorched by drought and then utterly stripped by the clouds of
insects which infested it from one end to the other. Description
of the land before the plague as a veritable Garden of Eden may
be something more than metaphor. All is pointing to the great
Day of the Lord, reaffirming his activity, and forecasting his determination to bring the sinful people to account. As "nothing
escapes" the locusts, so nothing—or, better, no one—will escape
his judgment.

Having drawn this comparison, Joel returns to a description
of the magnitude of the invasion of the locusts. It was no ordinary plague; it was the worst one the prophet and his generation had seen, and that very fact made it ominous for them. The
movement of the pests was like that of war horses proceeding in
orderly array—perhaps the head of the locust, shaped like that of
the horse, had something to do with the comparison, or the leaping of the locust which was like the gallop of a horse. In Job
39:20 the galloping horse is compared with the leaping locust,
and the writer of Revelation 9:7 likens the locusts to "horses ar-
rayed for battle." The rustle of their movement was like the
rumbling of chariots. Coming from the north (2:20), they
would naturally appear first on the mountains around Jerusalem,
whence they would descend upon the city like an army of horsemen. Not only could they be seen; they could be heard. The
sound of their ranks as they moved relentlessly onward was "like
the crackling of a flame of fire" (vs. 5) that devoured the stubble of the field in preparation for plowing.

Since such plagues were not unheard of in the land, the people were always fearful whenever they heard about locusts or
saw them, because they knew it meant famine or starvation.
Hence they were terror-struck at any sign of their presence; they
trembled with fear and grew pale (vs. 6).

Once more Joel turns to a description of the advance of the
locusts. They charge like an army, they scale the walls of city
and houses and go straight forward without turning to one side
or the other. Their course appears so well ordered that they never
go in one another's way. The worst feature of their onslaught is
that there is no known defense against them. Weapons have no
effect upon them, walls and doors cannot keep them out, and
shutters cannot bar them from house and home. The windows of
ancient houses were, of course, only lattices which offered no

problem to the locusts, because they could crawl right through them and penetrate to the innermost recesses of the home. Just as no human agency could restrain the locusts, nothing which men could devise could hold back the Day of the Lord or bar his judgment.

That appears to be the lesson drawn from the event by the prophet. Obviously he is dependent upon the prophecy of his predecessor, Zephaniah, whose oracles on the catastrophic character of the Day of the Lord still fill the reader with mixed emotions. He speaks of it as sweeping away "everything from the face of the earth" (Zeph. 1:2). While Joel does not speak in such unequivocal terms he does indicate the universality of the effect of that day. The references to the heavens and earth, the sun, moon, and stars, are broad hints of the universal character of the cataclysm envisaged by him. The Lord himself is in command of his host (the locusts), whom he has ordered into action. His army "is exceedingly great" and its purpose is the execution of his word. The inexorable forces of nature are under his jurisdiction and are employed by him to carry out his will and purpose. From the divine point of view the word is powerful enough to carry out its intent. From the human point of view, "the day of the LORD is great and very terrible," beyond endurance (vs. 11). All the pretentious barriers or defenses which man may erect, including preventive sacrifices and offerings, are not sufficient to ward off divine displeasure at a disobedient people.

A CALL FOR REPENTANCE

Joel 2:12-27

No prophet assumes the role of the Lord's man without some measure of hope. Even in cases where the message takes the form of direct warning of doom there is some feeling that there may still be a chance for repentance and consequent avoidance of the divinely threatened catastrophe. In fact, there would hardly have been prophets at all if such had not been the case.

A Call for Sincere Penitence (2:12-14)

This short but significant message breathes the spirit of hope; it is a hope that the full extent of the Lord's judgment may be averted or its effect somewhat mitigated by a sincere change of

heart on the part of the people, the rather small group of returned exiles. That hope is fortified by the word of the Lord himself. The words "even now" (vs. 12) indicate the fact that
though it is late, though the determination of judgment has already been concluded, as its prelude in the locust plague proves,
there is still the possibility of staying its full effect by proper action (see II Sam. 24:15-25). The first requisite for the realization of that hope was to "return to me with all your heart,"
which is the Hebrew way of saying "repent sincerely." The heart
in Hebrew thinking is the center of the *will* or what we would
call *mind*, as well as of the affections. Here the chief emphasis
falls upon the former. The people must set themselves to do the
will of the Lord. They must turn away from the indifference and
thoughtlessness so evident before the plague and turn back to the
zeal manifested for the Lord in the early days (see Jer. 2:2-3).
That return or repentance must be evidenced by "fasting, . . .
weeping, and . . . mourning," which were the outward signs of
genuine sorrow for sin (see 1:13-14). But the prophet warns that
to show mere external expressions of sorrow for sin is not enough.
He enjoins a deeper fasting, weeping, and mourning—that of the
heart. Unless the heart (the will) is rededicated, repentance is only
a meaningless formality (see Ezek. 36:26; Zech. 7:12). Nothing
less than a new heart was required by their dire situation (see Ps.
51:17). Here Joel strikes the note so strongly accentuated by the
other great prophets, that of a spiritual renewal which goes far
beyond ritual activities. Hence he calls upon his people to tear
their hearts and not just their garments.

The basis for Joel's hope rests on Israel's previous experience
with the Lord and the revelation of his character given to Moses
in Exodus 34:6 (see also Pss. 86:15; 103:8; 145:8; Neh. 9:17).
Both Joel 2:13 and Jonah 4:2 are based on that passage. But
much water had passed over the dam since the Exodus passage
had been written; not only had God's mercy and grace been
demonstrated at the time of the deliverance from Egypt, but in
the release from the Babylonian Exile they were even more apparent. Despite the sins which necessitated exile, forgiveness and
return were a far greater exhibition of grace than that shown to
Israel in Egypt. In addition there was his "steadfast love" abun-
dantly operative in the maintenance of the Covenant with Israel.
He was not a God who kept his anger forever. He was a relenting God and, if proper respect were shown for him and his way,

he might once again relent in the judgment he now decreed against the nation. The first sign of his forgiveness would be a blessing—the gift of food which the locusts had destroyed as the precursor of judgment still to come. The restoration of produce from the land would be a twofold blessing: food for the people and the means to provide cereal offerings and drink offerings as the recognition of their gratitude for God's forgiveness.

A Demand for a Service of Fasting (2:15-17)

To implement the call for repentance which he has just issued, the prophet enjoins the priests to "blow the trumpet in Zion" as a summons for the people to gather in a religious assembly to carry out the fast (2:15; see 1:14). Fasting was a common practice in times of calamity and was intended to express the humility of the worshiper before the judgment of God. The "solemn assembly" was a public religious convocation in which the whole community participated, as is indicated in the following verses. They are to gather the people and "sanctify the congregation," that is, bring them together into a sacred assembly. The assembly is to be all-inclusive. This represents the *extent* of the call to repentance, as verse 12 called for its *depth* and *reality*. Old men, children, and nursing infants are to be brought into the courts of the Lord. Even the bridegroom, who was generally excused from military or other civic responsibilities for a year (Deut. 24:5), and the bride were to be brought in. It was to be a real national convocation, brought together with the purpose of demonstrating a nationwide concern because of the judgment which had overtaken her.

When all have been assembled, the priests are enjoined to perform their particular function, which is to take their customary places "between the vestibule and the altar" (vs. 17), where they are to conduct a ritual of lamentation. The vestibule was in front of the main Temple, that is, to the east (I Kings 6:3), while the altar of burnt offering was directly before it (I Kings 8:64; II Chron. 8:12). The prayer they were to utter there is strongly reminiscent of the Covenant relationship between God and the nation. The plea is based on the doctrine of election whereby Judah (Israel) was peculiarly the Lord's and the Lord had pledged himself to keep and sustain the people. Sometimes that doctrine was pressed too far, but that can hardly be said in this case. Hosea had said that the Lord gave Israel food and clothing (2:8, 21-22), but what will the nations now say when his "heritage" is desperate for sustenance because of the plague? Hence they are to pray that the Lord spare his people from "reproach" and prevent them from becoming a "byword among the nations" (see Moses' prayer in Deut. 9:26-29). The worst thing that could happen to them was to be ridiculed by the pagan nations so that doubt would be cast upon the existence of their God (Micah 7:10; Pss. 42:10; 79:10). Especially would this be the case in the time of Joel, when the people were struggling for survival and their leaders had proclaimed their absolute confidence in God's will, power, and purpose for the reconstruction of the nation.

The Response of the Lord (2:18-27)

The Jealousy and Compassion of the Lord (2:18-19)

Apparently Joel had been successful in inspiring the people of Judah to repent sincerely, for here we are told that "the LORD became jealous for his land, and had pity on his people" (vs. 18). Obviously the promised deliverance which follows in verse 19 coincided with the first evidences of the abatement of the locust plague. The arousing of the "jealousy" of the Lord is brought about by the reaction of the nations who ridiculed his people (Ezek. 36:5-6) and consequently his rule. The other side of his jealousy was his compassion for his people which expressed itself in the blessings of restored produce in the land. The word "pity" is a bit weak here because it does not, in itself, suggest *action*, which the Hebrew implies (see Exod. 2:6; I Sam. 23:21; II Chron. 36:15). The Lord was stirred to action by the repentance of his people; his holy ardor was aroused on their behalf, and he did something about it. His compassion was his response in terms of bounteous crops. Verse 18 thus presents the fact of the result of the prayers of priests and people. The next verse reports on the response of the Lord, in the first person, and follows in thought directly after verse 17. It is in the form of a promise which, according to verse 18, had already been realized at least in part. The promise specifies the sending of "grain, wine, and oil," the staple products of the land. But it does not stop there; it points to a time when there will be no more "reproach among the nations," probably in answer to the prayer of verse

17. Thus the response of the Lord to the people's repentance takes the form of the elemental blessings of life together with security from the ravages of hostile powers.

Removal of the Invader or Locust (2:20-23)

Here is a vital part of the response of the Lord to the importunities of the priests and the people—the removal of "the northerner." The promise, often interpreted as referring to national deliverance, since the nation's enemies came mostly from the north (see Jer. 4:6), more likely refers to the locusts which descended upon the land from that direction. We must beware of reading too much into such passages; the whole of verse 20 is best explained as the promise of the Lord to drive out Judah's present enemies, which are the locusts, into the desert, into the eastern (Dead) sea and into the western (Mediterranean) sea. More recent locust plagues have operated in exactly the same way—driven into the sea by the wind, drowned, and then washed ashore in great heaps where they decayed and sometimes created a frightful stench followed by severe pestilence. Ridding the land of the locust, with the return of vegetation and the restoration of vine, olive tree, and grain, and the consequent arresting of the full judgment upon the people brought forth loud acclaim —"for the LORD has done great things!"—echoed in the refrain of the following verses (21-23), which is a little hymn celebrating the return of the blessings of life after a period of desolation and threatened starvation.

This hymn is really a song of thanksgiving expressing the joy of the land, nature, man, and beast for what the Lord had done. At the onset of the plague the prophet called for the sounding of the alarm because the "ground mourns" (1:10); now he calms the fears of land and people because the Lord has seen their plight and "done great things." Once more the land is summoned to rejoice and the beasts of the field are urged not to fear, because the pastures have been revived, fruit is appearing on the trees, and the fig tree and vine are bending low with their gifts. The "sons of Zion"—that is, the people of the land who are devotees of the Lord (see Ps. 149:2)—are also urged to join in the chorus of grateful song to the Lord, who has brought the early and late rain on the land as before—the pledge of good harvests and abundant life for the population. "The early rain for your vindication" (2:23) has, doubtless, a double significance, since

the word for "early rain" also means "teacher." The early rain
for "righteousness" again falls upon the earth in its customary
regularity because of the righteousness of God, or in accordance
with his Covenantal promise (Gen. 8:21-22). The play is on the
regularity of the rain and the righteousness of God, both operative in response to the repentance of the people and their restoration to Covenant fellowship. So much seems clear from the
words "as before" (see Isa. 1:26).

The Promise of the Lord (2:24-27)

What the restoration to the Covenantal relationship is going
to mean for the people is explained in the promises here recorded. First, there is the return of plenty to the land. The threshing floors will abound with precious grain and the oil and wine
presses will overflow with their products. What had been lost
during the fruitless years to the locusts, the "great army," will be
more than made up to the people. There will be more than
enough for man and beast, for they shall eat to their full satisfaction. Second, remembering the lean years, they shall "praise the
name of the LORD" (2:26). Praising him for what he had thus
done means to express their joy, probably in festivals of thanksgiving for the blessing of the harvest (see Ps. 149:3).

The third thing promised to the people is that "never again"
shall his people "be put to shame" (vs. 27). In the intercessory
prayer of the priests, as directed by the prophet, there was a petition requesting that they be spared the reproach of the heathen;
that is, the shame of being taunted with the words, "Where is
their God?" (2:17). Such a situation, says the Lord, will not
again arise, for he will bless his people so that the heathen will
have no occasion to taunt them. The repetition of this promise
in verse 27 points to both the sensitivity of the nation to such
ridicule and the certainty of the word of the Lord concerning it.
The constant reception of the blessings of the Lord will be certain proof that he is "in the midst of Israel," that he is upholding
the Covenant with them. That is the significance of the statement
"You shall know . . . that I, the LORD, am your God and there is
none else" (vs. 27).

SIGNS OF THE DAY OF THE LORD
Joel 2:28—3:21

The Outpouring of the Spirit (2:28-29)

The last five verses of chapter 2 (28-32) form chapter 3 in the Hebrew book of Joel, which has four chapters.

"Afterward" is both the connecting link with the previous verses and the beginning of a new oracle which stresses the fact that there is still more to come of the blessing of God. Gifts of food and drink are significant portents of the presence of God, but that fact will be even more evident "afterward," that is, in the time of the full flowering of the Day of the Lord for Judah. Such an outpouring of the Spirit of God will bring to realization the wish of Moses in Numbers 11:29: "Would that all the LORD's people were prophets, that the LORD would put his spirit upon them!" The origin of the prophecy is probably Isaiah 32:15 and 44:3; it is both expanded and contracted in Zechariah 12: 10, and it is universalized in Acts 2:17-21.

In the Old Testament the Spirit of the Lord is said to rest on judges (Judges 6:34), kings (I Sam. 10:6, 10; 11:6; 16:13), prophets (Micah 3:8; Isa. 61:1), and others with special aptitudes (Gen. 41:38; Exod. 31:3). Joel visualizes a time when special endowments by the Spirit are no longer essential, when all God's people will be endowed with his Spirit. He thus expresses the same hope proclaimed by Jeremiah (31:31-34) and Ezekiel (36:27-30). The vision of Joel extends to every person in the Judean community, to "all flesh," that is, "your sons . . . your daughters . . . your old men . . . and your young men . . . Even . . . the menservants and maidservants." Peter's address in Acts claims the fulfillment of this oracle in the sense of its realization and universalization which go beyond our prophet (Acts 2; see also I Cor. 12:13; Gal. 3:28; Col. 3:11; and especially Acts 10:45).

A feature which is often overlooked in the prophecy is the pronoun "my" attached as a suffix to the Hebrew term for "spirit." That signifies nothing less than the realization of that for which our Lord taught us to pray—"Thy will be done, On earth as it is in heaven"—except, as we should expect, its limitation here to Judah, as shown by the repeated use of "your."

Portents in Nature (2:30-31)

The portents herein mentioned are omens of the Day of judgment, the day of the destruction of evil in order that good may survive and flourish. The locust plague as described in the earlier portion of the book was such a portent. However, here the omens are extended somewhat and will appear in the heavens as well as on the earth. These signs are given as warnings of the impending judgment and are intended to call attention thereto. The description of the portents taking place on earth may indicate wars (as in Mark 13:7-8; see also Judges 20:38, 40) or natural phenomena accompanying the divine appearance (Ps. 18:7-15; Exod. 13:21-22). The portents in the heavens are also frequently associated with the coming of great events (Isa. 13:10; Ezek. 32:7; Mark 13:24; Rev. 6:12; see also Matt. 27:45; Mark 15:33; Luke 23:44-45). The character of the Day is evident from the adjectives used to describe it—"the great and terrible day of the LORD" (2:31; see Mal. 4:5); but Joel does not dwell on that phase of it. He is more concerned about the deliverance of Judah, of which these things are the signs.

Salvation for Those Who Call Upon the Name of the Lord (2:32)

To call upon the name of the Lord was to invoke him directly (see Gen. 4:26; 12:8; Pss. 50:15; 91:15). The breadth of the application of such an invocation is indicated by the phrase "all who call," and it appears to go beyond the community of Judah. Peter does not directly apply this thought in his speech at Pentecost but perhaps alludes to it in Acts 2:39 where he declares the promise to be to all whom "the Lord . . . calls to him," which may be a reference to the final clause of the verse. Paul does apply it in the wider sense in Romans 10:13. Joel thinks of escape for all who call upon the Lord in sincerity of heart, and to substantiate his belief he appeals to what the Lord has said according to Obadiah 17. "Those who escape" are the ones who do not succumb to the catastrophe which will overcome Jerusalem. In addition to them there will be others elsewhere in the land or perhaps out of it who have called upon the name of the Lord and whom he now calls to be with those who have escaped from the purifying judgment in Mount Zion and Jerusalem. Joel's prophecy probably looks beyond the time of restoration and re-habilitation of his day, even beyond Pentecost which marked the inception of a new age, to a time of the final consummation of things visualized by the writer of the Revelation in his announce-ment of a new heaven and a new earth.

Judgment for the Nations (3:1-8)

In the Valley of Jehoshaphat (3:1-3)

Chapter 3 is closely connected with the preceding verses of chapter 2, as is shown by the conjunction "for" which continues the description of the consequences of the Lord's judgment. "In those days and at that time" refers to the Day of judgment against the surrounding nations and deliverance for Judah. The prophet brings forth a new and more specific aspect of the mean-ing of the Day in what follows. The Lord will "restore the for-tunes of Judah and Jerusalem," which were at a very low ebb if we are to judge by the words of Haggai and Zechariah. There may be an immediate reference looking to a more propitious lot for Judah following the extreme poverty experienced during the first decades of the return from Babylon, and a more remote ref-erence having in view the distant period as in 2:28-29.

Judgment will begin when the Lord brings all the nations down into the valley of Jehoshaphat (since the fourth century A.D. identified with the valley between Jerusalem and the Mount of Olives and known in the New Testament as the valley of the Kidron). There is a play on the name of the valley which ap-pears only here in the Bible and which means literally, "the LORD judges" or "has judged." The appearance of the name here (the name of a king of Judah who reigned from 873 to 849 B.C.) may have something to do with the present position of the book in the Bible. In the valley of Jehoshaphat where the nations have been assembled for the purpose, the Lord will conduct a court of de-cision in which they will be tried for their treatment of his peo-ple, his "heritage Israel" (which is interchangeable with "Judah" in Joel).

The specific charge is that "they have scattered them among the nations, and have divided up my land" (3:2); that is, the na-tions were responsible for Judah's dispersion and the parceling out of the land. The same word here translated "scatter" is in

Esther 3:8 used to describe the dispersion of Jews throughout the world in the Persian period. But the reference here can only be to the Babylonian Exile, after which the land was taken over, at least in part, by other nations. Verse 3 is a further explanation of the treatment accorded the Judeans after the fall of Jerusalem. They cast lots for the survivors (see Obad. 11; Nahum 3:10) whom they then traded off for more desirable things. Dealing in human beings was particularly reprehensible, especially if they were sold into slavery (see Amos 2:6-7).

Judgment for Tyre and Philistia (3:4-8)

"What are you trying to do to me?" is the meaning of the introductory question of the Lord directed to Tyre and Sidon, the twin cities of Phoenicia, and to Philistia. "All the regions [districts] of Philistia" (see Joshua 13:2) refers to the five territories centering in the five cities of the Philistines. These nations or peoples were the most persistent opponents of Israel and are mentioned here for that reason.

The question has to do with any possible vengeance they may have in mind for injustice done to them by the Lord. Rather they merit the vengeance of the Lord for what they have already done to Israel (Judah). Any action they would take will be quickly answered by the Lord. Their guilt is laid bare in verse 5. They have carried off the possessions of the Lord by plundering his people (see I Sam. 5:1; 23:27; II Chron. 28:18) and have placed the booty in their temples. Other prophets and secular writers also denounced the Phoenicians for their dealings in human merchandise.

For the evil acts of these mercenaries there will be recompense. The Lord is about to awaken his people in the places where they have been sold by the slave traders, and when they return to their land the whole situation which existed when they were taken captive will be reversed. The shameful deeds of which they were guilty will be recompensed "upon your own head," that is, the measure they gave will be the measure they get (3:7; see Mark 4:24). As the sons and daughters of Judah were once sold to them, their sons and daughters will be sold to Judah which, as an intermediary, will deliver them into the hands of the Sabeans, who controlled the south Arabian trade routes in the sixth century B.C. Thus they will be removed to remote regions in the opposite direction from which they themselves were taken.

That was the pronouncement of the Lord and therefore as good as done; it was the judgment which they themselves had decreed.

Summons to Judgment (3:9-15)

Proclamation of War Against the Enemies of God's People (3:9-10)

The prophet takes us into the inner council of the Lord where the stage is being set for the great assize. We listen to the voice of the Eternal instructing the heavenly heralds to announce "this among the nations," that is, the following orders. First they are to "prepare [literally "sanctify"] war"—set in motion the sacrifice which marks the beginning of a military campaign (I Sam. 7:8-9; 13:8-10). Then the mighty men are to be awakened and the warriors are to be assembled and march up to the place of battle, to join in the fray. They are urged to provide for themselves weapons made from the implements of peace (the reverse of Isa. 2:4 and Micah 4:3), and draft into the army every possible wielder of arms. This is another way of saying what Amos said to Israel, "Prepare to meet your God" (Amos 4:12). The military terms employed to accentuate the seriousness of the conflict must not be allowed to obscure the real meaning. The judgment envisioned by the prophet will involve all the nations of the time; it will involve everything they can muster and it will be a desperate and decisive event, for even the weakest among their people will proclaim himself a warrior and participate in the fray.

Summons to the Nations (3:11-12)

The first word of the passage in the Hebrew is uncertain, and the translations are based on conjecture or on early versions. In any event, the nations around Judah are urged to proceed to and draw up for battle in "the valley of Jehoshaphat" (vs. 12), where the decisive conflict is to take place. The summons to the nations is followed by the request that the Lord also "bring down . . . warriors." The renewal of the summons to the nations to awaken and come to the valley of Jehoshaphat is now overshadowed by an altogether different figure, that of the court of judgment where the Lord sits to judge. Thus the figure of a great battle between the nations and the warriors of the Lord is joined to that of the nations gathered before the great Judge of all the earth.

The Harvest of Wickedness (3:13)

The heralds of the Lord are commanded to wield the sickle for the time is at hand, "the harvest is ripe." The judgment is frequently likened to the harvest ripe for the reapers (Isa. 17:5; Micah 4:12-13; Matt. 13:39). Harvest and ingathering of grapes with the activity of the wine press are commonly associated, because the latter regularly follows the former in the succession of the seasons. The wine press full for treading is another figure often employed with reference to the judgment (Isa. 63:1-6; Jer. 25:30). It is significant that, in contrast with this, the same figure is used in Joel 2:24 to depict the blessings of the Lord for his people, presumably after the judgment and following repentance and return to him. The ripeness of the harvest, the fullness of the wine press, and the overflowing of the vats with reference to the judgment is explained by the clause, "for their wickedness is great." The whole verse stresses the nearness of God's judgment.

The Application of the Figure (3:14-15)

In imagination the prophet already discerns the commotion of the hosts gathered "in the valley of decision" (see vss. 2, 12), which has a double significance here; that is, the valley where decision is about to be rendered, and that where the actual conflict is taking place. The tumult of the nations in the valley of decision is not accidental nor of their own volition; it is because they have been summoned there by the Lord, "for the day of the LORD is near." The tense of the verb in verse 15 suggests both the certainty and the proximity of the judgment. For the signs of the nearness of that Day see the discussion of 2:10.

The Redemption of the Lord (3:16-21)

The Lord on Mount Zion (3:16)

The dwelling place of the Lord is on Zion, from which he roars in judgment against the enemies of his people. Zion is parallel here with Jerusalem, as is usually the case. For the figure the prophet apparently draws on Amos 1:2. The terror struck into the hosts gathered against the Lord is implied here but noted elsewhere (for example, Isa. 29:6-8; 30:30-31). So is the destruction wrought upon them by his acts. The disheartening and ominous consequences of those acts upon his opponents are at the same time a reassuring sign to his people, whose refuge and bulwark he thus proves himself to be. The figures of speech are significant because they are associated with security, protection, and safety from the forces hostile to man.

Jerusalem (3:17)

Jerusalem as the dwelling place of the Lord will be demonstrated as such by these purging events. The Lord's people will know that he is indeed the Lord of all the earth and their God, because he has intervened on their behalf. This conception is probably based on Ezekiel, where the phrase "you shall know" appears scores of times and almost in the same general context of a mighty act of God illustrating or demonstrating his presence and activity. Jerusalem will be holy, and foreigners will not again "pass through it," that is, with evil intent and purpose. As the holy place of the Lord it is to remain inviolate in a physical sense. Joel was a Hebrew and possessed the characteristic spirit of realism which regarded history as the stage of activity of God. That means he viewed Jerusalem as the city of the Lord, and since it is, those who would defile it will be forcefully excluded, not just because they are strangers but because they are not interested in its welfare or are positively hostile to its God and people.

The Blessings of the Lord (3:18)

The extravagant picture of the fruitfulness of the land after the decision in the valley is like that obtaining after the repentance of the people following the locust plague (2:24). It is a figurative description of the blessing of the Lord in terms of the fertility of the land in the new age (see Amos 9:13). The usually dry wadies of Judah "shall flow with water" (vs. 18), another sign of the presence of the Lord with his people (see 2:23). The fountain or spring issuing from the Temple has Messianic significance and must be understood in the light of Ezekiel 47:1-12 and Zechariah 14:8. Those references with the one here are probably based on Isaiah 8:6 and probably show how the theme was developed and applied in exilic and postexilic times. See also the vision of the Revelator (Rev. 22:1-2), which marks a further expansion and application of the theme. On "the valley of Shittim" see the discussion of Amos 5:24. The passage is a glowing description of the salvation of the Lord attendant upon the conquest of evil and brought about by his mighty power. These blessings of a wonderful security and sustaining providence are the lot of God's repentant and delivered people.

Egypt and Edom Versus Judah (3:19-21)

Egypt and Edom were long-standing foes of Israel and in these verses may be regarded figuratively as the totality of her opponents. Since the Lord is a righteous God as well as a saving God, judgment falls upon his enemies while salvation is decreed for his people. Egypt had deceived Israel again and again, as the oracles of other prophets clearly indicate (Isa. 36:6; 30:3, 7), and Edom was always a treacherous nation (see the oracles against Edom in Jer. 49:6-22; Ezek. 25:12-14; Obad.), who took advantage of every opportunity to harass Israel. No specific allusions are offered us here, but the history of Israel is replete with instances of the perfidious acts of both nations, so that they become a constant symbol of hostility to her. In place of the fertile valley of the Nile, Egypt will become a desolation and Edom a forsaken wilderness. On the other hand, Judah, which had become desolate and forsaken through the instrumentality of enemies, will become prosperous and "inhabited for ever"; Jerusalem, as the capital, will continue "to all generations."

The last verse of the book is difficult in the Hebrew text. The Revised Standard Version reflects the Syriac and Greek versions and really is a summary of the preceding declaration. The people of Judah stand to be avenged or vindicated, while their enemies are declared guilty by what has happened to them. "The LORD dwells in Zion" is almost a signature of validity wherewith Joel closes his book. His final word is thus one of assurance of the supremacy and continuous presence of the Lord, and it reminds the reader of the last verse of Ezekiel—"The LORD is there." It is the most reassuring promise and truth of the Bible, comparable to the last word of promise of our Lord (Matt. 28:20).

THE BOOK OF

AMOS

INTRODUCTION

Authorship

The authorship of the Book of Amos has never been questioned; the herdsman and dresser of sycamore trees from Tekoa is, without a doubt, the real author of the oracles recorded therein. There are, however, as might be expected, other materials which, in one way or another, came to be associated with the genuine prophecies of Amos. Some of these were doubtless later applications to new but similar situations, others may have been floating traditions with some verbal similarities to Amos.

The author of the book was a resident of the kingdom of Judah, specifically of the fortified town of Tekoa about ten miles south of Jerusalem, five miles south of Bethlehem, on the road to En-gedi. It was the home of the "wise woman" (II Sam. 14:2) and of one of David's mighty men (II Sam. 23:26). Jeroboam I made it a fortified place (II Chron. 11:5-6), which status it probably retained till the days of Jeremiah (Jer. 6:1). The wilderness or desert of Tekoa is about twelve miles west of the Dead Sea, which is about 4000 feet lower in elevation. Around Tekoa were small plains where the shepherds kept their flocks and where a limited amount of agriculture could be carried on. At lower levels, toward the Dead Sea, were sycamore trees, which were cultivated to add to the meager fare of the population. The food supply was apparently always precarious, and the plagues (Amos 4:9-10; 7:1-2, 4), drought (4:7-8), and famine (4:6) of which the prophet speaks were doubtless familiar experiences to him. It was a hard place to live and nature was not very kind to the people there, but it did make for a type of rugged character which is displayed in the "wise woman," in David's hero, and particularly in Amos himself.

We know nothing of Amos apart from what is revealed in his book—but that tells us a great deal, not only of his occupation but of the man himself. His shepherd occupation gave him time for reflection and thought. The climate left its imprint on him, as did the rugged terrain. While he was a simple man, Amos was not an ignoramus. He knew about national and international affairs, he was deeply aware of the religious aberrations of his people, and he was steeped in the Covenantal requirements of the Lord. His persistent contemplation of all those things made him a man of profound convictions, as his prophecies indicate.

Date

The date of Amos is fixed, in a general way, by the super-scription which places his activities in the reigns of Jeroboam II (786-746 B.C.) and Uzziah (783-742 B.C.). The more definite reference given by the phrase, "two years before the earthquake" (Amos 1:1; see Zech. 14:5), is useless in assigning a date because we have no way of knowing, as yet, the year of that event. There are, however, some elements in the messages themselves which, in a general way, help us to arrive at an acceptable date. The dynasty of Jehu in Israel came to an end six months after the death of Jeroboam II, and the prophecies of Amos give every indication of having been delivered sometime before that. There is no hint of an immediate or impending danger to Jeroboam's rule, with the possible exception of the prediction of the uprising "against the house of Jeroboam" in 7:9. The overwhelming impression one receives from the book is that prosperity was general and the people complacent, which could hardly have been the case had there been internal difficulty or external danger. All in all, it is best to date Amos from somewhere around 752 B.C. to not later than 738 B.C.

Historical Situation

For details of the historical situation see the Introduction to Hosea, who was the younger contemporary of Amos and whose prophecies date from some ten to twenty years later. The historical situation in the time of Amos was somewhat more stable for the reasons stated above, but Amos was well aware of the fact that such stability could not last for long.

The Literary Formation of the Book of Amos

It is doubtful whether Amos *wrote* any part of the book which is called by his name. Although prophetic oracles (messages) were not unstudied and promiscuous deliverances, they *were* delivered orally and sometimes doubtless spontaneously (such an oracle is that of Amos 7:14-17). Like the words of Jesus, they were carried along in the memory of hearers, frequently for a considerable period of time, before they were finally "edited" or "collected" from various sources, just as today a biographer or editor of some other man's works collects his materials from written or oral sources. The Book of Amos is thus a compilation of messages and "visions" delivered by the prophet, probably during a short period, at Bethel and Samaria. Many of the materials are just as they came from the mouth of Amos. Others may have been placed into a context which may or may not have been the original context, and still others, which were part of the floating tradition, were placed where they now are out of other considerations.

In the first place there are the oracles of Amos which are, for the most part, contained in chapters 3 through 6, with a number of them in chapters 8 and 9. These oracles bear the stamp of authenticity because they deal with subjects which came under the observation of the prophet and which are treated in characteristic ways. They are introduced or concluded by the words, "says the LORD"—that is, "an oracle of the LORD (of hosts)"—2:11, 16; 3:10, 13, 15; 4:3, 5, 6, 8, 9, 10, 11; 6:8, 14; 8:3, 9, 11; 9:7, 8, 12. Or they may be introduced by "hear this word" as 3:1; 4:1; 5:1; or by "woe" as 5:18; 6:1.

Then there are the famous visions, five in number (7:1-3, 4-6, 7-9; 8:1-3; 9:1-4), which are certainly much as they came from the lips of Amos. Visions are characteristic of most of the prophets from Micaiah ben Imlah (I Kings 22) to Zechariah (Zech. 1-6).

There are also hymnal fragments which may have been included by the prophet himself. These fragments are in 4:13; 5:8-9; and 9:5-6, and in each case exalt the Lord because of his greatness and power.

Some of the materials of the book are couched in a form which has liturgical characteristics, as 1:3—2:16. The formula "Thus says the LORD: 'For three transgressions . . . and for four, I will not revoke the punishment . . . ' " is used eight times in the passage. The same rather formal character may be observed in the expressions, "Seek me and live" (5:4), "Seek the LORD and live" (5:6), and "Seek good, and not evil, that you may live" (5:14), though this may be simply a poetic device and not an accommodation to some aspect of the ritual. Also the dirge or lamentation in 5:2 is obviously a kind of hymn and so of liturgical character. Then there is the refrain, "Yet you did not return to me," in 4:6, 8, 9, 10, 11, which sounds like a liturgical imitation.

Finally there are some editorial pieces, such as 1:1-2a, portions of 7:10-12, and possibly some of the sections against foreign nations. Also some of the more specific applications may be an editorial effort to drive home the lessons of Amos for a later day and situation.

Purpose and Message

The purpose of the Book of Amos may be put into a single sentence: to preserve the message of the prophet whose name it bears. When one turns to the oracles and visions of the prophet himself, the intention is a bit different. His purpose was most certainly, first, last, and always, to deliver the judgments of the Lord to his people Israel (the Northern Kingdom). Prophetic pronouncement of judgment, however, did not consist simply in the utterance of threats. It consisted rather in the deliverance of the word of the Lord which, if obeyed, meant salvation or, if disobeyed, meant purging in some way or other.

And that is still the aim of the prophecy of Amos. It is to offer a clear-cut definition of the will of the Lord as it applies to the elemental relationships of life in a covenant of brotherhood. It is a clarion call to practice justice, which is right attitudes, thoughts, deeds, in every type of men's dealings with one another.

More specifically, we may select five paramount principles enunciated in the Book of Amos. First, and perhaps most important of all, is the prophet's emphasis on the universal dominion of the Lord, which had never before been so clearly and unequivocally stated, and which has ever afterward been assumed or been explicit in the prophets and in Christianity. The oracles against foreign nations (1:3—2:3) point quite strongly in that direction. The Lord has power over these nations, though it ought not to be overlooked that none of the great nations or empires are included. Later prophets did, however, include Babylon and Egypt and thus extend the idea of Amos. The most significant passage dealing with the concept is 9:7, a great affirmation of the equality of nations and the Lordship of Yahweh.

Along with the concept of universalism must be taken the rejection of the doctrine of election as privilege alone. Election, says Amos, is to service. The choice of Israel involved her response to the Covenantal offer of the Lord and bound her to him forever.

Amos emphasized social justice as a vital part of the Covenant responsibility. He put it so strongly and defined it so sharply that his name has forever after been associated in a special way with the concept. The justice which Amos demands is not just conformity to a civil code, though that is involved; it is much more the right dealings with and relationship toward others in the Covenant tradition.

Consideration of the quality of justice leads directly to a fourth principle which dare not be neglected in any treatment of the prophets, particularly Amos. It is the moral element involved in the Judeo-Christian religion. To the Hebrew, as well as the Christian, all life is sacred. God has something to say about the way men act toward one another, either within or outside the Covenant nation or group. Formal religion conducted at a holy place is not enough; indeed Amos feels that it is more often a hindrance than a help toward the fulfillment of the will of the Lord, because it tends to become a substitute for the "weightier matters of the law" (Matt. 23:23). Amos did not reject worship as such; he, with other prophets, was opposed to the incorporation of Canaanite elements into Israel's religion because it modified, sometimes apparently eliminated entirely, the principle of morality. It led to all kinds of immorality, indecency, and the practices of rites totally foreign to the ancient ideal of strict justice in the Covenant. And what was even worse, it seemed to confer a sort of religious license upon the worshiper, permitting him to act selfishly and inconsiderately toward his brethren when he had fulfilled his *formal* religious obligations. That Amos opposed uncompromisingly.

Lastly there is the direction which the prophet gave to the concept of the Day of the Lord (5:18-20). Hitherto it had been thought to be a Day for the vindication of Israel against her enemies. Amos regards it rather as a vindication of the word of the Lord, a Day of destruction for the wicked and all their associates. It applies to Israel as well as to her enemies because the

Lord is the universal God. So, instead of being a right royal Day for those who thoughtlessly conceived of themselves as specially privileged, it will be a Day of judgment, when the house of Israel will be sieved like grain until only the good grain will remain.

OUTLINE

The Date and Occasion of Amos' Prophecy. Amos 1:1-2

The Prophet (1:1)
The Word of the Lord (1:2)

Oracles of Judgment Against the Nations. Amos 1:3—2:16

Against the Aramean States (1:3-5)
Against the Philistine Cities (1:6-8)
Against the Phoenicians (1:9-10)
Against the Edomites (1:11-12)
Against the Ammonites (1:13-15)
Against the Moabites (2:1-3)
Against Judah (2:4-5)
Against Israel (2:6-16)

Some Sermons of Amos. Amos 3:1—6:14

On Israel's Responsibility (3:1-15)
On the Oppression of the Poor (4:1-13)
On the Lord's Judgment (5:1—6:14)

The Visions of Amos. Amos 7:1—9:15

The Locusts (7:1-3)
The Consuming Fire (7:4-6)
The Plumb Line (7:7-9)
Historical Interlude: Amaziah and Amos (7:10-17)
The Basket of Summer Fruit (8:1-3)
Judgments for Sin (8:4-14)
The Vision at the Altar (9:1-6)
Hope for Israel (9:7-15)

COMMENTARY

THE DATE AND OCCASION OF AMOS' PROPHECY

Amos 1:1-2

The Prophet (1:1)

The editor tells us in the very first words that here are the prophecies of Amos—he refers to them as "the words of Amos," a very effective way of describing the sermons of the prophet. The word of the prophet was the word of the Lord, and so the words of Amos were in reality the words of the Lord. The words of the Lord were often thought of as invested with personality; in this case they were incarnate in his prophet Amos.

The name "Amos" means "burden," and his full name was probably "Amosiah," the "burden of the Lord" (see the name of Amasiah, II Chron. 17:16). The home of Amos was Tekoa, some ten miles south of Jerusalem, in a narrow ravine surrounded by hills rising to more than 2000 feet, and overlooking the Dead Sea to the east. There he was engaged in the task of shepherding. The Book of Amos is a collection of what "he saw concerning Israel." The expression refers especially to his visions (see 7:12, where the term "seer" is applied to Amos by Amaziah, perhaps in derision).

The prophetic visions or revelations of Amos came during the reigns of Uzziah of Judah (783-742 B.C.) and Jeroboam II of Israel (786-746 B.C.). That is a very important fact which must be taken into account in any interpretation of the oracles (see the Introduction). More definitely his prophecy is said to have come "two years before the earthquake," which must have been a memorable event (see Zech. 14:5). Archaeology has revealed a stratum at Hazor in northern Galilee, dating from the period of Jeroboam II, which was destroyed by an earthquake; the city built on the rubble was subsequently destroyed by Tiglath-pileser III (745-727 B.C.).

The Word of the Lord (1:2)

In introducing the pronouncements of Amos, this verse

stresses the characteristics of the word of the Lord as well as its effects upon the nation as such. It may have been placed here by an editor as a kind of motto for the whole prophecy. Whatever its source, it certainly expresses the spirit of the prophet.

The formula is probably a very old one, emphasizing the power-filled word. The Lord roars like a lion, he thunders like the storm, and the pastures mourn and the finest vineyards wither. The origin of the word of the Lord is significant; it comes from Zion, from Jerusalem. That was, in the time of Amos and later, the residence of the word which is here said to have had devastating effect upon the land.

This was the creative and judging word which Amos was to transmit to the people of the Lord. It was a word that could remake Israel or destroy her, depending entirely on her response. All nature was moved by that word and felt the effects of its mighty declarations.

ORACLES OF JUDGMENT AGAINST THE NATIONS

Amos 1:3—2:16

Preceding the sermons of Amos is this series of oracles against the nations in the form of a prophetic liturgy. It is possible that some of the oracles have been expanded by the editor or transmitters, one or two could even have been inserted as a whole, but the general tenor of the material is so infused by the stern morality of Amos that it is not hard to believe that he was the author. Beginning as he did with a strong condemnation of other nations, he prepared the way for the word of the Lord to Israel. That was good psychology, because it aroused the interest and claimed the attention of the hearers. The prophecies were doubtless delivered at some festival which crowds of worshipers had gathered to celebrate.

Against the Aramean States (1:3-5)

The words, "For three transgressions . . . and for four," are part of the formal ritual pattern which opens each of the oracles against the nations. It must have been fairly common in Canaanite times since it occurs with variations relatively frequently in the literature of Canaan. It serves to indicate a succession of sins of which each accused was guilty. The "transgressions" were literally "rebellions"—against the Covenant structure of Israelite society—best illustrated in the oracle against Israel (2:6-8). Rebellions against the Lord's Covenant cannot pass with impunity; they have their own reward. "I will not revoke" (literally, "I will not make it turn back") means that God will not intervene in the outworking of the law of returns. The guilt charged against Damascus is that of extraordinary cruelty in one or more of her campaigns against Israel (see II Kings 8:12; 10:32-33; 13:7).

As might be expected, Damascus is referred to as "the house of Hazael" and "the strongholds of Ben-hadad" (vs. 4), both of whom were well-known kings and are often named in the Bible. "Fire" will destroy the palace and fortresses of the city, that is, war will level them to the ground. "The bar of Damascus" (vs. 5) in all probability is more than the gate of that city; more than likely it has to do with a league of Aramean states of which Damascus was the head. In the Assyrian inscriptions of the ninth and eighth centuries B.C., Damascus is frequently mentioned as the leader of a coalition of small states; and it was the prime mover later (than Amos) in the Syro-Ephraimitic War (Isa. 7). With breaking of the "bar of Damascus" will go the fertile valley of "On" between the Lebanon and Anti-Lebanon Mountains. The grasper of the "scepter from Beth-eden" was, in all probability, Shamshi-ilu, the power-crazy Assyrian governor of Bit-Adini, an Aramean state of the Euphrates, whose end was near when Tiglath-pileser III (745-727 B.C.) came to the throne. The exile of the Syrians (Arameans) came when Damascus was captured by the Assyrians in 732 B.C. (see II Kings 16:9), though the place of exile—"Kir"—is obscure. One important element in this and the following oracles is the concept of the universal dominion of the Lord and his determination to bring the nations to judgment for their wicked deeds and acts.

Against the Philistine Cities (1:6-8)

The second group of people to feel the sting of the prophet's words was Philistia. The Philistines were survivors of the days of Samuel and Saul, living in their cities along the seacoast to which they were confined by the conquests of David. Naturally they experienced numerous changes through the centuries, though not too adverse on the whole. The fact that "Gaza" stands for the group of five cities is of some importance, perhaps because it was the largest city, or because it was guilty in a special way of the crime with which it was charged. At any rate, all the Philistine cities are mentioned by name with the exception of Gath, which had been taken by Uzziah (II Chron. 26:6) but subsequently rebuilt, for it was captured by Tiglath-pileser in 734 B.C. and again by Sargon II in 711 B.C. The guilt of "Gaza" consisted of dealing in slaves, possibly as middlemen for the Phoenicians (vs. 9). To merchandise slaves was bad enough, as we shall see later, but to sell a whole population was almost unforgivable because there was left no seed for propagation. Edom was the recipient of the slaves but in the oracle against her is not condemned for it (vss. 11-12). We are not told who the slaves were, though some think they may have been Israelites. If so we can easily understand the bitterness of the prophet's denunciation of Philistia for carrying on such a traffic in human wares.

With the same formula as before, the prophet declares that the Lord is going to send "fire" against the walls of Gaza (see again II Chron. 26:6, where Uzziah is said to have broken down the wall of Gath) and "devour her strongholds" (towers). To "turn the hand against" means to smite Ekron again and again.

To the hearers it must have seemed as though the Lord was definitely on the side of Israel, and with one sweep of the hand would destroy her enemies. But assuredly Amos is here thinking of something other than an encouragement to Israel through the destruction of her political enemies. The Lord's judgment falls upon Philistia because her inhabitants have violated the most solemn covenant of human brotherhood, which follows upon the prophet's conception of the total dominion of the Lord. Because of their sin against the brotherhood of man, "the remnant of the Philistines"—that is, all of them, even beyond the cities named— will be punished.

Against the Phoenicians (1:9-10)

"Tyre" represents the Phoenicians who were themselves descendants of the Canaanites. In no sense does it refer to a distinct kingdom apart from Sidon at this time. Tyre was rebuilt in the twelfth century B.C. by the Sidonians and continued as the administrative capital of the Phoenicians until it was made into an

Assyrian province by Sennacherib (705-681 B.C.) early in his reign. The guilt of Tyre is the same as that charged against Philistia—"they delivered up a whole people to Edom," referring, in all probability, to slave trade (see Ezek. 27:13). In so doing, Tyre forgot "the covenant of brotherhood," or "the covenant of brothers." Solomon is called "my brother" by Hiram of Tyre (I Kings 9:13), and there were treaty relations between Tyre and Israel from the time of David (II Sam. 5:11; I Kings 5), and the Northern Kingdom had ratified a relationship with Tyre by the marriage of Ahab to Jezebel (I Kings 16:31-32). Despite these supposedly good relationships, later writers denounced Tyre severely (Isa. 23; Jer. 25:22; Ezek. 26-28; Zech. 9:3-4), though the situation had been greatly altered. It is likely that the writer's use of the phrase "covenant of brothers" furnishes a clue to the meaning he attached to his prophecy. He regarded violation of the Covenant as a transgression against God as the Creator.

Against the Edomites (1:11-12)

There was scarcely a time which did not see open hostility between Edom and Israel, although Esau (Edom) and Jacob were twins. Edom had been mentioned already in the two immediately preceding prophecies as the recipient of slaves, though in the time of Amos, Edom was apparently subject to Judah (II Kings 14:7; II Chron. 25:11-12, 19). The Chronicler (II Chron. 21: 8-10), however, speaks of an Edomite revolt against Judah in the reign of Jehoram (849-842 B.C.). Because of its shortened form, its position following the dual reference to Edom, and the fact that it reflects a time when Edom enjoyed ascendancy over Israel, this oracle may represent a later addition. Edom could hardly have exercised the cruelty here attributed to it before the last days of Judah (compare, for example, Jer. 49:7-22; Ezek. 25:12; Obadiah; which come from the early sixth century and which reflect the same bitterness voiced here).

The specific sins charged against Edom are the product of violence. The expression, "he pursued his brother with the sword," indicates the traditional family relationship, together with the suspicion which characterized that relationship in early times and probably continued to haunt both Israel (Judah) and Edom throughout their history as nations or even remnants thereof. Not only was Edom guilty of pursuing Jacob with the sword, but of complete lack of "pity," the feeling that ought to prevail among brothers, for the root of the word means "womb." Moreover, he cherished a lasting anger, born of jealousy, which was a complete negation of the Covenant. "Teman" was a province of Edom, possibly to the north of Petra; "Bozrah," modern Buseira, was somewhat less than halfway between the Dead Sea and the Gulf of Aqaba.

Against the Ammonites (1:13-15)

In contrast with the shorter oracles against Tyre and Edom, this one is fully developed. Ammon figured in Israelite history from the period of the judges (Judges 10-11; I Sam. 11; II Sam. 10-12; I Kings 4:21, 31; II Chron. 20:1; 27:5). From the time of David on, Ammon was more or less tributary to Israel or Judah and probably continued so until the westward movement of the Assyrians under Tiglath-pileser III, and the Syrian wars. At that time the Ammonites seized the opportunity of freeing themselves from the yoke of Judah, though they were compelled to pay tribute to Assyria. They obviously took further advantage of the situation to engage in expansionist activity. In the conduct of their forays they "ripped up women with child in Gilead, that they might enlarge their border," which means that they carried forward their intentions with cruelty and severity. The poet-prophet pronounces the same doom upon Ammon as he did for Damascus. "Rabbah" (Rabbath Ammon) was the capital city of Ammon, later Philadelphia and present-day Amman. Around the city will be heard the battle cry and it will be swept away as by a hurricane—"with a tempest in the day of the whirlwind" (see Jer. 49:2-3). Along will go "their king" and his officials. Complete destruction without hope of restoration is thus predicted for Ammon.

Against the Moabites (2:1-3)

Moab and Ammon, always closely associated, were said to have been the descendants of Lot by his two daughters (Gen. 19:37-38). Moab was located east of the Dead Sea; its traditional northern border was the Arnon River, but when not held in subjection it tended to expand northward. The profuse mention of Moabites in II Kings, Isaiah (especially 15-16), Jeremiah

(48), and Ezekiel (25) indicates their constant threat to Israel as well as their nature and strength on the political scene.

The charge against Moab is that "he burned to lime the bones of the king of Edom," a particularly heinous and vindictive crime. It implied not only the defeat of Edom but the relentless pursuit of the enemy to the cemetery and desecration of its supposedly inviolate tombs (II Kings 23:16). How serious this matter was may be seen from the many tomb inscriptions which pronounce terrible imprecations upon anyone who violates their contents. The "covenant of brotherhood" (see 1:9) pertains here too, though in a somewhat different manner. It is to be observed that there is no argument to establish a justification for the act or the punishment; the simple assertion requires no argument because its reprehensibility was recognized by all peoples at the time.

The same punishment is decreed for Moab as for the other nations who came under Amos' indictment. Fire, the purifying agent, will devastate Moab and its chief city, Kerioth, which, according to the famous Moabite stone, was the residence of the god of the nation, Chemosh. The judgment will be so violent that the whole nation will be in "uproar" and torn with strife. There will be shouting and alarm of war on every side so that convulsion will lay hold of the whole land. Not only will the land be devastated but her "ruler" and his officials will be slain so that there will be no possible opportunity for revival.

Against Judah (2:4-5)

The oracle against Judah is short like those against Tyre and Edom and is therefore sometimes regarded as a later insertion. It hardly seems possible, however, that Amos could have escaped mentioning Judah in his catalogue of the nations guilty of offenses against the Lord. If this portion of Amos is a later insertion, it shows how cherished and effective his prophecy was, even in subsequent times and in the south.

Judah is blamed in a very general way for despising "the law of the LORD," a phrase occurring in later literature but with a different meaning. The term used for "law" (torah) is found three times in Hosea, where it apparently refers to the moral injunctions of the Lord, his way, and his will, and four times in Isaiah (1:10; 2:3; 5:24; 8:16) with the same meaning. "Statutes" refers to that which has been set or engraved, and here refers to the moral teachings which became a vital part of Israel's law and which were well known. "Their lies," that is, their false gods, have entangled them and "led them astray." The punishment decreed for Judah is exactly like that decreed for the other nations. The same standard of universal morality is applied to Judah as to the other nations. There is no favoritism or leniency here.

Against Israel (2:6-16)

The Transgressions of Israel (2:6-8)

In harmony with what has just been said, Amos applies the same universal considerations of judgment to Israel as he did to the other nations, only he carries the conception of the Covenant of brotherhood a step further by demanding its observance within Israel. The specific violations of that Covenant fall like sledgehammer blows upon the heads of the guilty. There is a sense in which the charges are specified with remarkable clarity, and yet they are general indictments which are spelled out in detail later on.

"They sell the righteous for silver" (vs. 6) or they sell the legally blameless or innocent for silver; that is, they sell their own brothers into slavery or perhaps keep them in slavery for a longer period than was warranted by the circumstances. No Hebrew could be sold into slavery in perpetuity unless he willingly agreed to it (Exod. 21:2-6; Deut. 15:1-18; Lev. 25:39-46; see Neh. 5:8). Under the Covenant, slavery was abhorrent and for an innocent person to be sold for money was reprehensible. To sell "the needy for a pair of shoes" was even more detestable, for it indicates that those who were in need of food were sold for a mere token payment. Strictly speaking, such transactions were within the letter of the law but wholly outside its spirit. It is not difficult to see how, under such legal fictions, one could be held in slavery indefinitely, especially if he was a desirable slave.

Verse 7 deals with the attitude of the wealthy freemen toward the poor and less fortunate, as the preceding verse deals with brothers of the Covenant sold into and held in slavery. The rights of the poor would naturally be trampled into the dust where such low estimations of brotherhood prevailed. "The poor" here means the thin, those who were poverty-stricken by cruel circumstances, and hence helpless and without champions. Caring for them was always regarded as a particularly meritorious act (see Pss. 41:1; 72:12-13; 82:3-4; 113:7), because the Lord was concerned with them. The "afflicted" are those who have been humbled by their circumstances and so have no standing in the community. The rich took advantage of those who could not defend themselves or who had no one to plead their case before the elders.

"A man and his father go in to the same maiden," that is, they practice adultery in the most flagrant fashion (vs. 7). The emphasis falls not so much on the common practice of adultery as upon the regularity of the practice, as is indicated by the tense of the Hebrew verb. That is a profanation of the "holy name" of the Lord. If prostitution in connection with the practice of religion is involved, the situation is even more serious (see Deut. 23:17). Another interpretation, however, is possible. Change of only one consonant in the word for "maiden," a confusion quite frequent in the Hebrew, would give the word for "agreement." The meaning of the clause would then be, "a man and his father act by agreement," which fits well with the preceding accusations. Father and son regularly act concertedly to defraud the poor— a theme to which Amos returns repeatedly, whereas he has little to say elsewhere either about adultery or about sacred prostitution. On the other hand, "maiden" here may refer to a female slave whom both father and son used for their illicit desires.

The "garments taken in pledge" (vs. 8), which the law required to be returned before sunset (Exod. 22:26), were spread out for religious carousals beside every altar. Those garments which had been given as a pledge of payment to the creditor were thus paraded before the very altar of God, whose law had been violated. The wine unjustly extorted in fines they drank in the very sanctuary of "their God." Here are suggested two entirely different conceptions of God. Amos' God was a God of justice and righteousness, who demanded fair and honest dealings between brothers, as well as sympathy for those who were impoverished by adverse circumstances. "Their" religion was one which condoned all injustices in the name of legality. Caring nothing for their brethren, whom they should have helped, they thought only of themselves. It was a religion of the survival of the fittest, for they even sought to appease God, the spirit of whose law they had spurned, with the very materials—garments and wine—they had so thoughtlessly taken from the poor. Here, in unforgettable words, is set forth the difference between a religion whose chief concern is the Covenant of brothers and a religion of formality whose chief emphasis is on externals.

The Lord's Acts for Israel (2:9-11)

The God who is responsible for the maintenance of the Covenant of brotherhood was active in a peculiar way in the history of Israel. The supposedly indestructible Amorites had been removed from her way by the Lord. The Amorites here and in verse 10 are regarded as the pre-Israelite inhabitants of the hill country of Palestine (Deut. 1:7, 19-20; Joshua 24:15). To a helpless, unarmed people like the Hebrews coming out of Egyptian bondage, those inhabitants with their equipment, their prosperity, and especially their walled cities possessed a grandeur like the cedar and a strength like the stately and powerful oak (see Num. 13: 32-33; Deut. 1:28). But the Lord overcame them root and branch, prevailing over what appeared to the Hebrews as insuperable obstacles.

Amos begins with the conquest of the land and moves back to the mighty deliverance from Egypt, rather than the reverse, as is the case with many of the great writers of the Old Testament. Verses 9 and 10 in the Hebrew both begin with the emphatic pronoun "I" which, of course, refers to the Lord. Speaking through Amos his prophet, the Lord says, "*I* destroyed . . . *I* brought you up." The direct intervention of the Lord is stressed to point out the power of God working for his people. No man or nation had resources and strength enough to operate against the most powerful empire in the world at the time. Yet Israel's God prevailed over the Pharaoh and his hosts, led his people out of Egypt, and cared for them in the period of their wilderness wanderings. He it was who also assisted them in taking possession of the land of the Amorites. In recalling this strategic period of history, Amos emphasizes what the Lord *had* done for his people in the past and indirectly indicates what he can and will do for them now, if they obey him or permit him to do so. But their recent actions reflected little recognition of the Lord and certainly no understanding of his gracious and powerful deeds.

God did not leave his people alone. He raised up "prophets" and "Nazirites" for them, to guide them and to bring them his will and teaching. The prophets were the called of God to proclaim his word to specific situations, men such as Gad, Nathan,

Micaiah ben Imlah, Elijah. The Nazirites were the separated ones, those who followed the simpler and more austere desert ideal (see Num. 6 for the Nazirite law). These dedicated ones were a living protest against the paganizing of Israelite life.

Attitude Toward Teachers (2:12)

The prophet goes on to describe the utter contempt in which these teachers and separated persons were held by the luxury-loving people. Though there is no record of a specific instance of such forced degradation or even of temptation offered the Nazirites, one can easily see how some of them had been misled (see Jer. 35:5-10). But there were attempts to silence the prophets who spoke in the name of the Lord (for example, see Amos 7:12-13). Many of them were treated severely, and, later, one was murdered by an angry king (Jer. 26:23-24; see also the tradition referred to in Matt. 5:12; 23:30-35).

Inescapable Judgment (2:13-16)

The theme of these verses is "Be sure your sin will find you out." The figures of speech which the prophet employs to convey the Lord's judgment are extraordinarily effective and realistic— terms which every Israelite farmer and villager would have understood. The unrighteous are going to groan, as a cart, heavily laden with grain, groans when it is taxed to the limit of its strength; before the threshing floor is reached it collapses under the weight. Or, as the Revised Standard Version suggests, their sin renders them like a heavily laden grain cart which cannot make progress (on the way to the threshing floor) because of the weight pressing down upon it. Israel is loaded down with transgression as a cart is loaded with sheaves.

The nation is in a situation from which there is no escape. The fleet of foot cannot get away in flight, strength fails the mighty, and even the warrior is impotent to save himself (vs. 14). When the enemy attacks, the forces of the nation will disintegrate because there is no stability there; they will be like an army without a general, sheep without a shepherd. The bowman cannot stand to draw his bow, the runner's feet will fail him, and even the horsemen will stand petrified before the invader (vs. 15). The most courageous warrior will flee naked, stripped of armor and implements of war, "in that day" (vs. 16; see 5:18-20).

SOME SERMONS OF AMOS
Amos 3:1—6:14

On Israel's Responsibility (3:1-15)

The first sermon prepares the way for what follows. It is as well oriented psychologically as the oracles against the nations had been. There the central point was the universal dominion of God and the Covenant of brotherhood which applied to all nations and for which they will be brought to judgment. Here the theme is judgment upon Israel for its defection from the Covenant of election-love whereby the nation had been given a definite responsibility.

Election and Responsibility (3:1-2)

Amos is the purveyor of the word of God to the "people of Israel," that is, the people of the Northern Kingdom. It is not his word but God's word, and is directed to them specifically. The second portion of verse 1 is an editorial expansion and the later application of the prophecy to "the whole family which I brought up out of the land of Egypt." The reader must remember the immediate audience the prophet was addressing, though his words were applicable to his own people of Judah, and indeed to us. But Amos was speaking to a specific group in Israel at a specific time and place. The editor has drawn the proper conclusion by reminding us that Amos' word of the Lord is based on the mighty deliverance from Egypt and therefore rests on the Covenant.

The stern reminder of verse 2 is the "text" of the sermon. Israel's election rested on the free choice of the Lord. He had entered into a special relationship with Israel because of her early response to his overtures. That relationship is defined by the words, "You only have I known of all the families of the earth." The word for "know" means far more than our translated term. It here means "to choose," that is, to select because of intimate acquaintance with (see Hosea 13:5); it signifies the familiarity which exists between persons who are intimately aware of one another. The Covenant is based on such knowledge and was essentially an offer of grace (Exod. 34:6-7), because Israel had no particular qualifications to claim the Lord's attention (see Deut. 7:6-11). But the offer of grace and love brought with it a corresponding obligation, a responsibility to be his people (Lev. 19:2; 20:7, etc.). Israel was chosen to be the servant of the Lord. Election of grace spelled service in his name, though such service was itself a privilege. Because of the Lord's act of grace in choosing Israel, she was on familiar terms with him; she was the recipient of the revelation of his will and purpose. The very fact that she had such intimate knowledge made her subject to more severe judgment than others who did not know. That principle was stressed by our Lord when he observed, "Every one to whom much is given, of him will much be required" (Luke 12:48). Israel knew the way of the Lord; therefore, says Amos, she is responsible and will be brought into judgment for all her "iniquities," that is, her deviations from the way.

Cause and Effect (3:3-8)

No stranger could make such dire predictions as Amos made without being questioned about his right to speak. These verses are manifestly intended to show that his prophecies are not idle words; they have been called forth by a just cause.

In a series of challenging questions, therefore, the prophet presents his credentials which are voiced in verse 8. The first question (vs. 3) is based on the personal experience of the prophet in the lonely region of Tekoa where persons going in the same direction would hardly meet except by appointment. There is purpose in Amos' word to Israel; he has been sent by appointment and does not speak promiscuously. The prophet had doubtless often heard lions roar and had observed that they never do so without having taken prey; nor do the young cubs in their lair cry out when they have taken nothing (vs. 4). The snared bird is trapped by the net or the bait set for it in the net (vs. 5). A trap is not sprung without cause. Ancient traps were so constructed that they would not go off without taking a victim, although the prey might not be held. When the watchman on the city walls sounds the alarm of approaching danger, the people of the city respond with trembling (vs. 6). The people were all familiar with the examples offered by Amos and would have answered each question with a resounding "No." None of these things could have occurred without a cause. Amos, too, was "caused"; he was there because of the call of the Lord.

Verse 8 brings the whole series of questions to a point and applies them to the situation confronting Israel. The prophet was not deceived by the prosperity of the nation under King Jeroboam II. Whereas the people had taken the veneer of success as the real thing, Amos was aware of a wider orbit of political movements stirring in the world of his time, and he knew that a people as debauched as Israel could not withstand the onslaught when it came. The lion of Assyria was roaring and he trembled; the Lord God was speaking and he had to convey his message to Israel.

How did Amos come to recognize the word of the Lord as the people of Israel did not? That is explained in verse 7. Not only was he aware of the movements of the great colossus from the north—Assyria—but he stood in the intimate council of the Lord. Jeremiah's observation was that the false prophets had not stood in the intimate "council of the LORD to perceive and to hear his word" (Jer. 23:18), and so their predictions were their own fabrications and not the word of the Lord. According to the Psalmist that council was revealed to "those who fear him" (Ps. 25:14), that is, to those who reverence and obey him, who keep his Covenant. Hence the prophet was more than an ordinary person; he was the messenger of the Lord par excellence, one who knew his will, purpose, and plan and who spoke with divine authority. He was God's man of the hour; what he spoke would come to pass, unless the conditions of his warnings were met.

Samaria's Arrogance and Its Reward (3:9-11)

The heralds of the intimate council of the Lord are to cry from the towers of "Assyria" (the Septuagint translation; see margin) and of Egypt the Lord's invitation to the nations to assemble themselves to the mountains of Samaria to see a strange and unexpected sight. Here was a nation with unparalleled prosperity and a devotee of the great God who is the Lord. But what would the spectators see when they took their seats in the Israelite national theater? Two outstanding features, almost characteristic, would be apparent at once. One is what the prophet calls "the great tumults within her" (vs. 9). That is, despite the material advances and blessings of the time there was great unrest and a sense of insecurity everywhere. The second feature evident to the onlooker is "the oppressions in her midst." The oppression rampant in Samaria was extortion, seizure of the possessions of others.

Actually matters had come to the point where "those who store up violence and robbery in their strongholds" "do not know how to do right" (vs. 10). They could no longer discern the true way of the Lord and hence were incapable of functioning under the Covenantal standard. All their vaunted prosperity had impoverished the nation by coming between the people and the Lord, and between themselves and their brethren of the Covenant.

Material prosperity often saps the vital strength of a people so that they become spineless and impotent in crises that demand virtue, effort, and valor. That was precisely the situation in Israel. The "adversary" (vs. 11) is bound to come against such a land. When the blow falls upon Israel it will not be a light one; her defenses will be demolished and her fortresses plundered. Arrogance is weakness, and has its own recompense in times of stress.

The Relentless Pursuit of Sin (3:12)

Amos does not hold out much hope for deliverance. Israel had become so incapable of doing right that there was little chance ·of change. The figure used to describe the situation which will prevail is drawn from the prophet's experience as a shepherd. The flock was often invaded by a wild beast which would snatch an unsuspecting sheep from the flock and make away with it. All that was left when the shepherd caught up with the marauder was the leg bones or the ears. Not much consolation for the shepherd! Only here and in 4:11 is the idea of deliverance present in Amos—but what a deliverance it is! For only insignificant bits of Israel with its erstwhile glories will be rescued from the hands of the invader—"the corner of a couch and part of a bed." Only archaeological remains will bear witness to the presence of a once prosperous people.

An Oracle of Doom (3:13-15)

Again we are transported into the council of the Eternal where the command is issued to give attention to and testimony against "the house of Jacob" (vs. 13). The speaker is the Lord himself, the "God of hosts," the Mighty One, in whose hand is the destiny of men and nations. The word of the Lord is clear and devastating. The expression "on the day I punish Israel" does not point to a fixed day on the calendar of God, but to the certainty of the coming of such a day of visitation because in the economy of the Lord it could not be otherwise. The "transgressions" of Israel (see 2:6) will be punished. The word "transgression" here means rebellion against the will and way (Covenant) of the Lord. "The horns of the altar" which the inadvertent transgressor might seize (I Kings 1:51) and where, according to the law, the blood of atonement was smeared (Exod. 30:10), will fall to the ground because there will be no use for them; they will no longer serve as a place of asylum, nor will there be atonement available for them. "I will punish the altars of Bethel" is an explanatory addition which designates the particular altars meant.

The oracle of doom is directed chiefly against the magnates of Israel who, in the prophet's mind, were the chief sinners of the nation. Not only did they participate in the commercial activity of the day, in the great bazaars of the mercantile centers of the world, but they were profiteers. They used their wealth for self-aggrandizement and to gratify their desire for luxurious living; they had winter houses (literally "autumn houses") and summer houses (literally "harvest-houses") which, says Amos, will be cut off. An inscription dating from this very period has the complaint of the writer that, unlike other princes, he has only one house for summer and winter (see also the reference to Ahab's palaces at Jezreel, I Kings 21). In addition, these would-be aristocrats had ivory-panelled houses (I Kings 22:39). Excavations at Samaria have disclosed many ivory carvings and panels which were doubtless originally used in the royal palace or in the houses of the officials and well-to-do people of the city. Such luxuries were the style of the day for the wealthy, as we know also from excavations elsewhere in Syria and north Mesopotamia.

Thus what Amos saw was the houses and extravagances of the rich on the one side and the hovels of the poor on the other. That was a violation of the Covenant of brotherhood *within* Israel, and as such was deservedly condemned. Apparently the most striking thing about the whole affair was an attempt to justify the situation on the basis of prosperity, to interpret it as a sign of the blessing and approbation of the Lord.

On the Oppression of the Poor (4:1-13)

Feminine Luxury (4:1-3)

The oracle begins with an indictment of the women of Samaria whose incessant demand for luxuries had compelled their husbands to look for ever-expanding sources of income. The belles of Samaria are likened to the "cows of Bashan" (vs. 1). Bashan was the grassy region on the east side of the Jordan and north of the Yarmuk River, known for its fine herds (Deut. 32:14; Ezek. 39:18). The cows of Bashan were fat and well groomed, celebrated for their sleekness and excellent proportion. Here is exhibited the unwholesome activity of the magnates of Samaria who crushed the poor of the land because every day their insatiable wives kept calling, "Bring, that we may drink!" Apparently there was competition not only in commercial enterprise but also among the families of the capital as they tried to outdo one another in parties and feasts (the literal meaning of "drink").

The judgment with which Amos threatens them is a most solemn one, introduced by the words, "The Lord GOD has sworn by his holiness" (vs. 2). There is another "Lord" who has something to say to the lords of Samaria. The cry of his people who are oppressed and defrauded, deprived of their living, weighs more heavily with him than do the inordinate cries of the "cows of Bashan." The mixture of gender in the Hebrew of verse 2 indicates the extent of the judgment about to overtake all the people of Samaria. Both men and women stand guilty before the Lord. As the real cows of Bashan were led with hooks, so these people will be led away captive with hooks in their noses. There are Mesopotamian monuments depicting captives led away by their captors by just such means, which furnish visible illustration of the prophet's words. Even to the last one of them, will the captor come. The present ruins of Samaria show how right he was.

Verse 3 continues the figure begun in verse 1. Each one will go out through the breaches of the broken-down walls of the city as cows go out one by one through the gate of the enclosure which confines them. The last clause of the verse is uncertain. The reference to "Harmon" is totally obscure. Some translations have "dungheap" or "refuse pile"; one commentator suggests "naked." Either or both may be right because some term of opprobrium is obviously intended. In any case, the coming experience for the women of Samaria will be just the opposite of that pertaining when they were in their glory.

Samaria's Religion (4:4-5)

This is perhaps one of the most bitterly ironical passages in the Bible. The oracle may have been delivered on the occasion of a religious festival at Bethel; it is directed to a wide circle of worshipers and not just to a particular group as was the case with the preceding one. Almost madly the prophet cries out in effect: "Come to Bethel and sin, at Gilgal sin still more! Bring your daily oblations and your tithes; offer your sweet-smelling, leavened thank offerings, announce voluntary offerings, advertise them—for that is what you love." Bethel was one of the two central shrines of the Northern Kingdom; Gilgal was the old, historic shrine (Joshua 4:19, 20; I Sam. 7:16). Amos' words were almost like an invitation to "Go to church and sin" (see Jer. 7:1-14). The prophet's words do not mean that these things were necessarily wrong of themselves—though there is a strong hint of the human origin of the mechanics of religion in the pronouns, "*your* sacrifices" and "*your* tithes," and in the person of the verb "for so *you love* to do." What he means is that religion for the people of Samaria is a caricature, a travesty, and has no deep spiritual content or significance. Oblations, tithes, offerings, have become nothing more than a substitute for true Covenant religion (see Jesus' words in Matt. 23:23). The formal observances had become an easy way to pay what they took to be their obligations to the Lord, and were a cloak for their daily inhuman practices toward their brethren. Here Amos was dealing with one of the most fundamental problems of all religion—that of the place of the mechanical aspects of religion. Amos saw clearly that a series of ritual performances can be no substitute for "the weightier matters of the law." That is just what the worshipers at Bethel had made of their Covenantal trust. Ritual is a mechanical device which may be helpful, beautiful, and symbolical, but it is not and can never be an end in itself; it must always remain a means to an end. Otherwise it is simply idolatry.

Unheeded Warnings (4:6-11)

The Lord not only instructs his prophets (3:7), but through them and through historical events he attempts to warn and direct his people. He never lets his people perish without witnesses to his way and will (Acts 14:16-17). Amos points to lessons given to Israel from time to time for the purpose of influencing them to return to the ways of the Covenant.

One of the most common occurrences in Palestine is famine ("cleanness of teeth"), which is the subject of the first pronouncement (vs. 6). While there is no definite indication of a particular famine, the words "in all your cities" hint that it was nationwide. The parallel statement, "lack of bread in all your places," reinforces the whole concept of a general calamity. Once more we have the first instance of a refrain which recurs several times in the chapter—"yet you did not return to me" (vss. 8, 9, 10, 11). The famine did not produce the desired results of repentance and return to the way of the Lord. His visitations, whether in grace or punishment, were always for the purpose of salvation and of bringing sinners back to relationship with himself (see Hosea 14:1; Isa. 10:20-23; Acts 3:19; I Thess. 1:9).

Another frequent occurrence and one which is antecedent to famine is drought (vss. 7-8). We are reminded of the great drought in the time of Ahab and Elijah (I Kings 17-18) which had a devastating effect on the land. The prophet speaks of the winter rain which usually begins in October and continues until about February. Failure of this rain or its early cessation works havoc with staple crops. "Three months to the harvest" points to the premature end of the winter rainy season whose results could not be altogether alleviated by the spring rains. Water is one of the most precious commodities of the land; the location of villages and towns made it imperative that the precious liquid be stored up in cisterns for use in the seasons when wadies and streams were dry. The storage facilities were sufficient, generally, only for local citizens, which meant that little could be spared for others; indeed, often it had to be severely rationed for the residents themselves. Hence it was that when "two or three cities wandered [literally, "staggered"] to one city to drink water" they could rarely be given enough to slake their thirst. Calamities of drought also did not cause them to "return" to the Lord.

Along with drought go "blight and mildew" (vs. 9). The word translated "blight" really means "scorching" and refers to destruction of crops by the searing, burning wind which blows its hot breath across the land from the desert. Its effect is to blight vegetation, sometimes in a single day. In its wake follows mildew, a kind of rust which covers grainfields and causes immense damage to the grain. The two terms, "blight" and "mildew," occur together in the Hebrew also in Deuteronomy 28:22; I Kings 8:37; and Haggai 2:17. Locust plagues (vs. 9) were also common (see Joel) and could be most destructive. The shearer type of locust is mentioned only here and in Joel 1:4 and 2:25. But again these natural visitations did not lead to a return to the Lord.

The Hebrew word for pestilence (vs. 10) occurs about fifty times in the Old Testament, which indicates its relative frequency in the thought if not in the experience of the writers. The reference here is to pestilence as a form of judgment. The latter portion of the verse has to do with war, often associated with pestilence. On "the stench of your camp" see Isaiah 34:3. One cannot read the story of Israel without becoming aware of all the troubles which Amos recalls to the thoughtless worshipers at Bethel. In any event, they still refused to return to the Lord.

Verse 11 seems to refer to an earthquake, as indicated by the mention of Sodom and Gomorrah which were destroyed by a similar catastrophe (Gen. 19), although some interpreters think the words "a brand plucked out of the burning" connect it with destruction wrought upon Israel by the Syrians in the reign of Jehoahaz (II Kings 13:7). The second word for "overthrow" is used elsewhere only of the destruction of the Cities of the Plain which was caused by an eruption believed to have been due to an earthquake. Moreover, Amos has referred generally to natural events with their devastation, and it is hard to believe that he would have singled out a particular battle for special comment in view of the fact that he referred to war in the preceding verse. But whether the event was an earthquake or a tragedy of war, Israel did not recognize in it the hand of God endeavoring to bring her to her senses. She still refused to repent and return to him.

The Judgment of the Eternal (4:12-13)

Famine, drought, blight and mildew, locust, pestilence, war, and destruction of cities did not interrupt the nation's persistence in apostasy, its failure to renew genuine Covenantal religion. The refrain—"yet you did not return to me"— which runs through the whole chapter tells the story. Now one more opportunity is presented to the people: the preaching of the Lord's prophet. Events preceding the activity of Amos had failed to bring about repentance and renewal but this last event—the giving of the word—is offered before judgment overtakes them. "Thus I will do to you" (vs. 12) does not refer to the judgment which befell Sodom and Gomorrah, but rather points forward to yet other judgments still to come, perhaps more devastating and severe. Amos calls for preparation to "meet your God," which has a double meaning because of the nature of the Lord's judgment. The call is for readiness to face God for repentance or for destruction, depending on the response to his offer.

Verse 13 is in all probability a wisdom-saying portraying the glory and majesty of the God who is the author and purveyor of judgment. The mention of the formation of the mountains and the creation of the winds reminds the reader of certain passages in Job (for example, ch. 38). The word for "forms"—as a potter forms a vessel—is used in Genesis 2:7, 8, 19, and in the later writers the word for "creates" is employed of God's creating (as in Gen. 1:1) as over against man's making of things. The Lord who is the Creator has not left man in the dark, for he "declares to man what is his thought," that is, God's thought, probably through the prophets (see 3:7). The God who brings forth the dawn to dispel the darkness and rides across the hills in thundercloud is the Lord God of hosts.

On the Lord's Judgment (5:1—6:14)

Lamentation for Fallen Israel (5:1-3)

The discourse begins with a lamentation for Israel, notice of which is given in verse 1. Because he knew what was about to happen if the people continued to reject the will of the Lord, Amos sang to the assembled worshipers a lamentation over the fall of Israel. A lamentation is a well-constructed dirge expressing sorrow and disappointment over the occurrence of an especially untoward event (as, for example, the so-called Lamentations of Jeremiah, which mourn the fall of Jerusalem and the captivity of Judah). There is a special lamentation meter in Hebrew, used here and in Lamentations, in which each line has three plus two beats. The consternation that was aroused in the crowd as the old prophet took up his solemn chant in this formal lamentation meter can be imagined. He was pronouncing doom upon the nation and, while it had not yet come, it was as good as done. Amos sang the funeral song for Israel while she was still alive.

The dirge is short but to the point. Amos refers to the nation as "the virgin Israel" (5:2), and thus reminds us of Hosea whose prophecy is based on the same theme. This is actually the earliest representation of Israel as a woman (maiden) and doubtless is the ultimate origin of the idea of the Church as the Bride of the Lamb (Rev. 21:9). In any event, Amos pictures Israel as a fallen virgin, one who has forfeited her virginity by her illicit relationships with lovers other than the Lord (see Hosea 2:5-13).

In the catastrophe of judgment her lovers cannot save her; in fact, they will desert her, and no one will "raise her up" (vs. 2).

The prophet interprets the meaning of the dirge in verse 3, which points to invasion as the manner of judgment. The extent of the catastrophe is nothing short of calamitous, for ninety per cent of the population will be destroyed. While this particular pronouncement is not predicated directly on a cause, it is obviously based on the refusal of the people to hearken to the word of the Lord.

True Search for the Lord (5:4-5)

Despite the coming judgment, the Lord never gives up seeking the reconciliation of his people. Hence Amos announces what must be done to save the nation—"the house of Israel"—which is addressed directly in verse 4. What is required for life? "Seek me and live" is the answer. To seek the Lord is to care about him, to respond to his saving love. (See Isaiah 55:6; Psalms 34: 10; 69:32; 119:2; the sayings of our Lord in Matthew 6:33; 7:7; and the parables of Luke 15.) To maintain his existence Israel must hear the word of God, respond to his call, and return to him, which will mean a revitalization of the Covenant.

Seeking God and living is set in contrast with attendance at the religious centers of the land: Bethel, Gilgal, and Beer-sheba (vs. 5). This is one of the most amazing contrasts in the Book of Amos and rests on a perceptive experience far in advance of the time. Already in 4:4-5 the prophet had characterized the religious practices as a mere caricature, but here he makes a contrast between indirect and direct religious experience. The whole tradition of Israel's religious life centered about cultic practices, and such important places as Bethel, Gilgal, and Beer-sheba were hallowed by the most sacred associations of the nation. Beer-sheba went back, as a sacred place, to patriarchal times (Gen. 26:23-33), as did Bethel (Gen. 28:10-22; 35:1-15). Gilgal, too, had been venerated since early times (Joshua 4:19-20; I Sam. 7:16; 10:8; 11:14-15). But now Amos advises the people not to go there. Why? Because the worship had been taken over by agricultural rituals with their excesses, which were far removed from the pure religion of the days in the wilderness, which seems to have been the ideal of the prophets. The sacred high places had become hotbeds of sin, as Amos declared (4:4-5). This marked a tremendous step forward in the conception of man's relationship with God. It implied a relationship without altar, cultus, or any other media—a conception which was well understood by the prophets but which the people in general could not comprehend for lack of experience.

The Lord Who Alone Has Power to Save (5:6-9)

In the preceding passage a contrast is set forth between seeking the Lord and attending the cult centers of the day. They will vanish but the Lord is a living God who remains with his people. Here another reason is cited for seeking him—to preserve the nation from savage destruction. The fire that devours is the fire of judgment sent to remove the evil so that the good may survive and prosper. In the case of the "house of Joseph" (the Northern Kingdom) the fire will consume the dross, the impurities of sin. Since the whole house stands guilty, obviously not much will be left. Certainly Bethel, the chief religious center, will be impotent to quench that consuming fire. The sin is that they turned "justice to wormwood, and cast down righteousness to the earth" (vs. 7). Instead of the sweet relationship of justice which should have obtained among the people of the Lord, there was the bitter wormwood of illicit and unjust acts. This rather severe judgment of Amos is confirmed a few years later by Hosea (see Hosea 4: 1-3).

The interlude of verses 8-9 is in a form typical of the Wisdom Literature. It reminds the people of the Creator and Orderer of the universe whose will they are flouting. The "Pleiades" (literally, "heaps of stars," the so-called seven stars) are mentioned only three times in the Old Testament—here and in Job 9:9 and 38:31. Orion (see Job 9:9; 38:31) was a bright constellation, observed very early because of its brilliance. Because of the connection of both constellations with the rising and setting sun they marked the seasons of the year. But they were under the control of the Lord who made them and placed them in their orbits. God also is responsible for the seasons, for the turning of darkness to light and day into night. "Deep darkness" is the same word used in Psalm 23:4 and there rendered "the shadow of death." The reference here is not to Sheol (the abode of the dead), as often supposed, but to the deepest kind of darkness, as dark as the tomb. The Creator of the seasons is also the bringer of the dawn, and the night of rest following the feverish activity of the day. More than that, he is the one who waters the dry, hard earth.

"The waters of the sea" which are poured out "upon the surface of the earth" (vs. 8) may refer to the heavy rain of autumn which sweeps over the land to water and fertilize it, or to the inundations of the river valleys which have the same effect.

The mighty God of nature and the universe is also the governor of the moral universe, the structure of society. There he exercises his power with equal order and certainty. He flashes destruction "against the strong" (vs. 9), that is, upon those who appear invincibly strong to men. The ruler of the universe is capable of overcoming those who set themselves up as gods and who rule from the fortified palaces.

Injustices (5:10-13)

Amos now reverts to the problems discussed in verse 7, where he lamented the fact that justice and righteousness were perverted so that the Covenant was dishonored. Here he takes us to the city gate where the cases of law were heard and judgment was rendered. The reference to "him who reproves" (vs. 10; see Isa. 29:21) is to the advocate who argued the case or who pronounced judgment. The one "who speaks the truth" is the member of the council of elders who stands and speaks for the right. The people who try to dispense justice and who reprove wrong are hated and loathed by those who think they stand above the law or are determined to follow their own desires, no matter how many people are hurt thereby. The real focus of religion for Amos was the city gate where the contests of life were resolved.

The word "therefore" (vs. 11) introduces the divine observation on this situation. The word for "trample" in all probability has a double significance—to exact exorbitant rent from the poor, and to trample them still further down into misery. "Exactions of wheat" were demanded by the rich landlords who farmed out the land to local tillers of the soil. Such exactions were forbidden by law (Deut. 23:19). It is difficult to say how many portions of the produce of the soil had actually to be paid out, but no doubt several were required. The whole method and practice of land-rent must have been outrageous or there would not have been such a violent protest on the part of the prophet. Out of the proceeds of their unfair and certainly unbrotherly dealings these extortioners "built houses of hewn stone," that is, well-constructed and luxurious homes of costly materials. The poor farmer was compelled to live in houses put together with field stones. But those who had constructed the more permanent and costly houses would have no advantage, for in the coming destruction they, too, will be destroyed. Nor will they be able to enjoy the "pleasant vineyards" which they have planted; for they will disappear.

The Lord who knows all things and who tries the inmost recesses of the heart of man (I Chron. 29:17; Pss. 7:9; 11:4; 139:23; Jer. 11:20; 17:10) cannot be duped. He declares, "I know how many are your transgressions, and how great are your sins" (vs. 12). Transgressions are failures to attain Covenantal standards. These rebellions and sins are described in the lines that follow. Men oppress the innocent, or those declared legally to be in the right; and they take bribes to acquit the guilty, a practice specifically forbidden by the Law (see Exod. 21:30; Num. 35:31). Those who could afford to pay bribes went free, while those who could not do so were held guilty. Thus justice was unequally applied, another practice forbidden by the Law (Deut. 16:18-20). Hebrew law was especially considerate of the poor and needy, but this principle was also violated as ways and means were found to "turn aside," or to prevent, the right judgment from being executed whenever it was in favor of the poor.

The effect of such handling of justice in an "evil time" (vs. 13) will cause the prudent man to keep silent. He is aware of the fact that, though justice may be on his side, he will not be treated fairly and so he refuses to go to the city gate with his case. The result is that wrong goes unredressed and righteousness is suppressed. Such heaping up of wrong upon wrong cannot go on forever, especially in the Covenantal community. Surely it is an evil time when it is wiser to keep silent and endure injustice than to bring one's complaint to the attention of the court.

Call for Justice in the Gate (5:14-15)

Turning to the positive side of what he has just said against those who pervert human relationships, Amos urges all the citizens of Israel to "seek good, and not evil," that they may live (vs. 4). Twice before he has emphasized that admonition, perhaps as a kind of text in his sermon on the Lord's judgment. The term "seek" applies to both good and evil here, with the implication that the people were actually seeking evil, perhaps quite unaware of the ultimate outcome of their actions. They were thoughtless of others and careful only for their own interests, oblivious of the effect of their deeds upon others. The prosperity which they enjoyed appeared to be evidence of the presence and help of the Lord. But, says the prophet, if they really desire that presence of the Lord they must seek the good; that is, be even more concerned about that which is right and good than about themselves.

If they act positively and with determination, the promised judgment of the Lord may yet be averted, at least in part. If they "hate evil, and love good" and, in consequence, "establish justice in the gate," he may relent and "be gracious to the remnant of Joseph" (vs. 15). The "remnant of Joseph" can refer only to the future and not to the present. Nothing that Israel can do now will totally avert judgment, but perhaps some of the nation will be spared (see 5:3). The chief stress falls on a definite change of attitude and emphasis in religion as the dynamic force within the nation and in its application to human relationships. That is the meaning of hating evil, loving good, and the establishment of justice in the gate. The word for "justice" refers to the outworking of the common law of the land, governed and determined by the Covenant of brothers.

National Mourning (5:16-17)

Not much can be hoped for from Israel, according to this word of Amos on the coming lamentation. He begins with "therefore" (vs. 16; see also vs. 11), which points backward to the basis for the following declaration. But that basis is actually unexpressed; it is in the mind of the prophet who, in view of the self-satisfaction of the people, does not expect them to return to the Lord. The social and religious context in which he is speaking made that conclusion inescapable, and the people to whom he was delivering this oracle understood perfectly what the situation was, so that there would be no doubt as to the meaning of the prophet's words. He was declaring to them the mind and purpose of God who knew what the popular reaction would be but who also had the power to fulfill his word, as the phrase "the God of hosts" shows. In a sense this is a return to the theme of lamentation with which the chapter began. When the blow fall "there shall be wailing" in the plazas of the cities and towns everywhere the cries of "Alas! alas!" will be heard, for the mourners will be confronted not only with the death of people but also with the death of a nation. The seriousness of the calamity, as Amos sees it, is indicated by the fact that the farmer will be called to participate and professional mourners will be

summoned to take their accustomed places. In times of great
sorrow, such participants always responded to increase the solem-
nity of the situation. Even in the vineyards which customarily
resounded with songs of joy at the time of vintage, there will be
mourning and wailing (vs. 17). The Lord himself "will pass
through the midst" as he once passed through the land of Egypt
to slay the first-born of the Egyptians, an event which called forth
the most violent lamentation (Exod. 12:12, 30).

The Day of the Lord (5:18-20)

This is one of the most far-reaching and celebrated prophecies
of Amos. The concept of the "day of the LORD" may originally
have been connected with royal festival celebrations marking the
enthronement of the king as God's representative, though it is
uncertain how far such rites were actually carried out in the
Northern Kingdom. The idea was probably associated with the
Day of the victory of the Lord over his enemies (see Exod. 14:
30; Joshua 10:12-14; Judges 4:23; I Sam. 3:12; 14:23; Isa. 2:12;
Hosea 1:5, 11). The theme was then taken up by Amos, Hosea,
Isaiah, and especially Zephaniah (see Zeph. 1:2-18), and applied
to the coming judgment upon the nation for its wickedness.

The victory of the Lord was a popular idea, acclaimed loudly
at religious festivals. The people thought of it as a grand and
glorious day, when the Lord would defeat and destroy all Israel's
enemies, and give her the privilege of rule, and shower upon her
all the material advantages her patriots desired. But Amos gives
the whole matter a new turn. The Day the people desire and
clamor for will be one of "darkness, and not light" (vs. 18).
These are symbols for adversity and prosperity respectively. That
Day will be one of judgment for themselves rather than for their
enemies. Only for a morally righteous nation could it spell blessing and life; it could mean deliverance only for those who were
unjustly oppressed and deprived of their rights.

There can be no escape from the hand of the Lord on that
Day (vs. 19). It will be as if a man escaped from a lion only to
be met by a bear, or fled to the supposed protection of a house
and breathlessly steadied himself by placing his hand against the
wall, only to have a poisonous serpent bite him. The Day of the
Lord will be one of certain doom for disobedient Israel. It will
be a day of utter darkness and gloom, a day with not so much
as a ray of light for the wicked nation which did not know God

(vs. 20), a day altogether different from that earlier day when he delivered them out of Egypt.

Condemnation of Formal Religion (5:21-25)

This passage is one of the severest condemnations of heartless religious formality in the Bible. Observe that this is not simply the judgment of Amos; the Lord is the speaker, of course, through the mouth of Amos. But there is no "thus saith the Lord" here. This is one of those instances where the Lord clothes himself with the prophet (see Judges 6:34; II Chron. 24:20).

The religious and political leaders had apparently hoped to gain the favor of the Lord by the strict observance of formalities and fat sacrifices. It was as if God himself stood by the altar that day and in the midst of the sacred ceremonies cried out against the very thing they were doing: "I hate, I despise your feasts, and I take no delight in [literally, "I loathe the smell of"] your solemn assemblies" (vs. 21). The supposedly sweet-smelling sacrifices were stench in the nostrils of the Eternal, because they came from corrupt hearts and foully intentioned minds. Even the "burnt offerings and cereal offerings" (vs. 22), the commonest and most frequently offered oblations (Exod. 20:24; 32:6; Judges 20:26; I Kings 3:15), are rejected as a means of appeasing the Lord. These offerings were designed to serve as a visible means of confirming reconciliation to the Lord, offered by those who had sinned inadvertently and were genuinely sorry for their sins (see Lev. 1-4). But such was not the purpose of the offerings of these people, and the Lord will have no regard for them.

We know relatively little of the actual instrumental or vocal music which accompanied the sacrifices at this period, particularly in the Northern Kingdom. In the time of Hezekiah there were musical guilds and professional singers at Jerusalem, as we know from an Assyrian account which records the fact that Sennacherib accepted male and female singers as tribute from the king of Judah. Hymns were undoubtedly employed in the worship at Bethel, and Amos implies an elaborate system of worship conducted at the sacred places in the northern shrines. But he asserts that, in view of the unholy practices of the people, those sacrifices were nothing more than a tumult, a lively noise, and he calls for their cessation. Not only do the supposedly sacred songs sound like so much noise, they are actually a burden to the Lord, who demands that they be removed from him. He refuses to listen to the "sound" of their harps. They thought that they would be heard for their high-sounding rituals, but in that they were as mistaken as the Gentiles were in the assumption that they would be heard in prayer "for their many words" (Matt. 6:7).

What then is acceptable to the Lord? The Psalmist declared, "The sacrifice acceptable to God is a broken spirit; a broken and contrite heart, O God, thou wilt not despise" (Ps. 51:17). Out of such hearts would issue deeds commensurate with the will and Covenant of God. The Lord looks for sacrificial lives, not empty sacrifices. That is what Amos affirms in the declaration which may be regarded as the central affirmation of his prophecy. Earlier (5:15) he demanded the establishment of "justice in the gate." Similarly, in 5:24 "justice" is the right decision in the simple cases at the city gate. It must be as plentiful and refreshing as the waters rushing down the wadies of the land after the early rains, and as persistent as the perennial streams that form the sources of the Jordan.

The final verse of the section (5:25) is in prose but it can scarcely be doubted that it comes from Amos. It is to be noted that whenever the prophet speaks of sacrifices he says *your* burnt offerings, *your* songs, and *your* harps, as much as to say these are their ways but not God's (see Isa. 55:8-9). Some interpreters hold that the Hebrew sacrificial system developed in Canaan and was not a part of the religion practiced in the wilderness. It is true that the prophets generally seem to regard it as an intrusion which came in with the settlement of the land and with prolonged contact with the Canaanites. "When you come to appear before me, who requires of you this trampling of my courts?" Isaiah demands to know (Isa. 1:12; see vss. 13-17). And Jeremiah expressly says, "For in the day that I brought them out of the land of Egypt, I did not speak to your fathers or command them concerning burnt offerings and sacrifices" (Jer. 7:22). These strong expressions do not, however, necessarily mean that the prophets thought of sacrifices as absolutely wrong, but that they thought of them as misused and, therefore, a hindrance to true devotion to the Lord. Whatever interfered with such devotion or was interposed between the Lord and his people was wrong and had to be removed. Amos looks upon the experience in the wilderness as reflecting the proper relationship between Israel and God, so that anything that militates against its realization in the land is unworthy and sinful.

Exile for the Disobedient People (5:26-27)

These verses are illustrative of the influence of pagan cults in the west in the time of Jeroboam II. "Sakkuth" and "Kaiwan" were probably images in human form representing certain celestial deities, and were carried around in religious processions. Amos recognized the origin of such abhorrent practices in the words, "which you made for yourselves" (vs. 26). They were not gods in themselves, nor could they, by any stretch of the imagination, represent the Lord of whom no image was to be made. Emotional extravagances of a morally bankrupt people led to all sorts of improvisations in religion, including processions of all kinds. Their processions will lead directly to the place where such activities are practiced—"into exile beyond Damascus" (vs. 27). Amos promises Israel exile in a land which carries on the kind of religion and life her people seem to love.

No Security in Samaria (6:1-3)

Here the prophet turns his attention to the proud boast of security in Samaria, a claim which must have been heard on every side, particularly after Jehoash's defeat of Amaziah (II Kings 14:11-14). The Indian summer of Israel's prosperity accentuated a feeling of pride, and fostered the arrogance of nobles and rulers alike. The pronouncement of woe upon those who feel secure in Zion (vs. 1) probably has a double reference; it recalls the security felt by Amaziah of Judah in the fortress and religion of Zion at Jerusalem and also the similar trust which the people of Samaria had in their own religious system. The twin fortresses of security and protection upon which every nation in history has relied are military fortifications and religion. Both can be deceptive, as Amos indicates, for both are only what the people make them. While the Hebrew of the second part of the verse is obscure in the details, it seems to continue the thought of the preceding by directing attention to the nobles who are in charge of affairs at Zion and Samaria. The meaning of the whole passage then appears to be that strongholds, shrines, and personnel in control are no guarantee of security for any nation or people.

As historical examples, evidently well known to the people to whom Amos is speaking, Calneh, Hamath, and Gath are cited (vs. 2). Calneh, to the north of present-day Aleppo, was incorporated into the Assyrian empire by Tiglath-pileser III. Hamath was the center of an Aramean principality which figured constantly in the coalitions against Shalmaneser III. Gath was also an object of Assyrian campaigns, and was taken by Uzziah of Judah in the time of Amos (II Chron. 26:6). It is not mentioned with the other Philistine cities in Amos 1:7-8. The instability in the west before the time of Jeroboam II makes it impossible to determine the particular situation to which the prophet refers. Certainly the cities are held up as examples of those who trusted in themselves but who, when the fatal hour struck, were unable to withstand the onslaught of their enemies. The crucial question is, "Are they better than these kingdoms?" That question strikes right at the heart of Israel's conception of herself as the chosen of God (see comment on 3:2). Amos places no confidence in the privilege of election claimed by a self-righteous nation whose life could not be distinguished from that of so-called pagan nations.

As a result of complacency brought on by the peculiar interpretation of election, the people "put far away the evil day" (vs. 3). They scorned the thought of disaster, as may be seen from their response to the sermons of Amos (7:12-13), and continued in their evil ways. "The seat of violence" points to the wrong which governs their national and social life.

The Besetting Sin of Luxury (6:4-8)

The age of Jeroboam II and his predecessors in the Northern Kingdom could well be called the "ivory age," for the whole Syrian and north Mesopotamian world gives evidence of its use. Carved ivories were highly prized and were often an important item of tribute or spoil received from subject or conquered peoples. The couches (vs. 4) were inlaid or decorated with ivory panels, often with religious motifs. How could the wealthy barons of Samaria procure such luxuries? By the oppression of the poor and defenseless people of the land. Their carousing also revealed a carefree, unconcerned attitude, especially regarding the underprivileged. They were not satisfied with the fare of the common people but ate "lambs from the flock" and stall-fattened, tender cattle.

Along with such elaborate feasts went entertainment. They sang "idle songs to the sound of the harp" (vs. 5). The Hebrew indicates improvised songs, songs that came to mind on the spur of the moment, adding to the debauchery of the occasion. They even considered themselves as skilled as David in the invention of instruments of music. Another interpretation has been suggested for this part of the verse, which rests on a slightly different division of the Hebrew consonants, without a change of the actual text. It is that when the celebrants were overcome by food and wine they took their jugs and fists for musical instruments, upon which they "doodled," utterly unaware of the incongruities.

That such an interpretation may be correct appears from the following verse. The charge that they "drink wine in bowls"— large vessels employed in religious ceremonies (Exod. 27:3; I Kings 7:40; II Kings 12:13)—accentuates the excesses in which they indulged. A further mark of their extravagances is their use of the choicest cosmetics, "the finest oils." Olive oil was widely used after bathing as a mollifying agent against the fierce heat of the sun, but perfumed oils were reserved for the rich (I Kings 10:10; Ezek. 27:22). Anointing with oil was customary on festival occasions and was the symbol of joy. Its use for that purpose is not condemned here, but the prophet does condemn the use of costly oils purchased at the expense of those defrauded.

The revelers are not concerned for the "ruin of Joseph." Herein lies the crux of the situation. The fact that they have luxuries in abundance while their compatriots have nothing shows the "ruin" of Joseph, the wound in the body of the nation. There can be no resistance when the enemy attacks this nation, with many of its people starving and the rest overfed and obese.

The self-indulgent will be the first to go into exile. They count themselves "chiefs" and chiefs they shall be—the chiefs of those who are taken captive (vs. 7). The depth of the prophet's emotional reaction to the high life of Samaria on the one hand and to oppression and injustice on the other is shown by the last verse of the section (vs. 8). God will not permit himself to be ridiculed by those who so shamelessly disregard his Covenant. Therefore he swears by himself (elsewhere only in Jer. 51:14) to the declaration that follows. As certainly as he himself exists, the Lord abominates the pride of Jacob, that is, his vanity, his affluence, his trust in material power. The "strongholds" which he hates are the fortifications which were designed to protect the nation and which became substitutes for trust in the Lord; perhaps there is also reference here to the well-appointed mansions of the rich, which would harmonize well with the preceding statement about the pride of Jacob. The Lord has determined to "deliver up"—to abandon—the city, together with its contents.

The Coming Destruction of Samaria (6:9-14)

Verses 9 and 10 describe further the desolation and destruction about to overtake Samaria. The stern judgments pronounced by Amos grew more severe. In 3:12 he speaks of the rescue of some from the city, in 5:3 he indicates that ten per cent of the people (or army) might escape, but here he expresses almost no hope for any deliverance. Even the "ten men" remaining in a house shall die, perhaps of pestilence following the devastation of war. Whole families will perish, so that only near kinsmen are left here and there for the clean-up operations. They burn the bodies of the dead—a practice not common among the Hebrews —to avoid further contamination. If, perchance, one is found hidden "in the innermost parts of the house" and inquiry is made of him about possible survivors, his only response is a muffled "No," which is to say, "I am all that is left." Moreover, such fear has taken hold of him that not only is he afraid to talk but he forbids the use of "the name of the LORD," lest the wrath which had already wrought such terrible destruction fall on him.

Verses 11-14 continue the prophecy of doom which is to overtake the city because of its sin of luxury and pride. The phrase, "the LORD commands" (vs. 11), emphasizes the fact of direct causation characteristic of the Old Testament. The Lord can both create and destroy. He commands and the result appears, either creation (see Ps. 148:5) or destruction (as here). At his command "the great house shall be smitten . . . and the little house," that is, all the dwellings of Samaria will suffer equally.

The following rhetorical questions bring out the utterly unreasonable conduct of the nation in the light of their knowledge of God and his commandments. In the nature of things horses do not run upon the steep, rocky mountainsides; they can perform only on roads or level ground. Nor does one "plow the sea with oxen" (vs. 12). That is not only unnatural but impossible. Yet Israel had done what was palpably even more unreasonable and unnatural. The supposed guardians of "justice" (what is right in human relationships) had turned it into poison. They thus made the very foundations of the Covenant suspect, and created mistrust in the hearts of those seeking redress of wrong. Their unjust decisions had turned justice into a mockery and thus had poisoned the whole system of judicial recourse. Every decision served to make the whole process more unpalatable. They turned "the fruit of righteousness into wormwood." What could be expected to be the wholesome bread of righteousness became bitter in the hands of those who judged and rendered decisions for their own benefit, or for that of their friends, or for a bribe.

The straws to which these thoughtless people cling are expressed in the prophet's reference to "Lo-debar" and "Karnaim" (vs. 13). It is not impossible that a double significance was attached to those terms. Lo-debar was a small town in Transjordan, near Mahanaim (II Sam. 9:4, 5; 17:27); Karnaim may be connected with the Ashteroth-karnaim of Genesis 14:5, or the Karnaim of I Maccabees 5:26, a town in Gilead where some of the followers of the Maccabees were incarcerated nearly six hundred years later. It may be that Amos is referring to the conquest of two small and relatively insignificant towns on the other side of the Jordan which had been hailed by the patriots of Israel as an indication of their national strength. In any case, Lo-debar (literally "no-thing") is nothing to brag about, and its capture did not require much strength (Karnaim is literally "strength").

Verse 14 forms an effective conclusion to the oracles of chapters 5 and 6. It brings to a focus the judgment pronounced upon Israel and virtually specifies the nation which is to be the "rod of the Lord's anger" (see Isa. 10:5) and the methods it will use. The nation which is to be raised up "against you" (the phrase indicates that no new nation is meant but one which already existed; that is, Assyria) will be directed to proceed against Israel. The construction in Hebrew shows that the movement had already begun. This nation will oppress Israel from "the entrance of Hamath to the Brook of the Arabah," the extent of the land established by the conquests of Jeroboam II (II Kings 14:25). The word "oppress" is often used to indicate subjugation over an extended period of time (Exod. 3:9; Judges 4:3); it literally means to squeeze or crush. Such will be the lot of the nation which rejects instruction, which obstinately trusts in her own strength, and which operates through unjust courts at the city gate.

THE VISIONS OF AMOS
Amos 7:1—9:15

The visions of Amos in the last three chapters, broken only by the historical sketch of 7:10-17, reinforce the ideas already put forth by the prophet in direct address. They are introduced, for the most part, by the words, "the Lord GOD showed me" (7:1, 4, 7; 8:1), but 9:1 begins with the simple statement, "I saw the LORD," which sharpens that particular vision. Here the speaker turns to symbolism in a further strengthening and justification of his message. The visions are, in a sense, autobiographical and as such suggest the basis for the oracles Amos has delivered.

The Locusts (7:1-3)

The phrase, "the Lord GOD showed me" (7:1), which marks the introduction to the first vision, is used to introduce other prophetic visions (see Jer. 24:1; Zech. 3:1). The verb is literally "caused me to see," and refers to knowledge based on experience. The experience in this case was observation of a locust plague in the process of formation. The type of locust specified is uncertain, but may be either one that appears suddenly or one that is in the larva stage. "The beginning of the shooting up of the latter growth" was in all probability the second crop, upon which the people depended for their own use after the king's tribute had been paid. In that case a locust invasion would be doubly catastrophic because they could hardly rely on any relief from the political authorities.

When the locusts had devoured all the green herbage, and the prophet became fully aware of the consequences, especially as they affected the common people of the land, he implored the Lord for forgiveness (vs. 2). The land of Jacob was small and had few resources, despite the boasts of the nobles. If such calamity should continue for long, Jacob could not stand. So the Lord relented (literally, "was sorry" for his people). The idea of the Lord's repentance is expressed a number of times in the Bible (see Exod. 32:12; Joel 2:13; Jonah 3:10). God said, "It shall not be" (vs. 3). Amos thus held forth the mercy and forgiveness of the Lord, which were available to the people until the very last. The only reason for his proclamation of destruction was the persistent rebellion of Israel.

The Consuming Fire (7:4-6)

The second vision vouchsafed to Amos in the council of the Lord was concerned with a much more severe judgment. It had to do with a "judgment by fire" (vs. 4). The word "judgment" refers to the Lord's case against the people (see Isa. 3:13; Jer. 2:9; Hosea 4:1; Micah 6:2). For a parallel to the idea of judgment by fire see Isaiah 66:16. The figure underlying the vision is that of a vast and destructive conflagration breaking out in the dry season and consuming everything in its path (see Joel 1:19-20). So enormous was the heat and consuming force of the fire that it "devoured the great deep" upon which the earth was believed to float and from which issued the springs and fountains of the earth. The blast of such a fire was so great that it threatened to lick up even "the land" (literally "the portion") which the Lord had provided for the people. This judgment is more extensive than that of the locusts, because it divested the people not only of food but also of water, the most essential element for life in the land. Once more the prophet intercedes for Israel, on the same grounds as before but with a much stronger word. "Cease" is an almost commanding appeal, voiced before the Lord. Again the Lord "repented" or was sorry for the lot of his helpless people. The almost complete lack of defense on the part of the people before locust and fire ought to have convinced the most intractable and obtuse of them that they could not stand before the awful judgment of the Lord, and that without his help it would be impossible to live. In the same way the Lord's relenting in the execution of his judgment should have confirmed his willingness to forgive the most violent sinners, if they turn from their wickedness.

The Plumb Line (7:7-9)

The third vision was inspired by the observation of a house wall accurately constructed with the aid of a plumb line (or plummet). Here Amos saw the Lord standing with a plumb line in hand, and he heard his voice asking, "What do you see?" (vss. 7-8). The question affords an opportunity for the interpretation of the symbol. The purpose of a plumb line is to determine the perpendicular accuracy of a wall, in the same way that a level is used to determine the horizontal accuracy of a foundation. (For similar usage of the symbol see Isaiah 28:17; II Kings 21:13.) As applied to Israel it signifies that the Lord is in the act of applying the plummet test—the test of the standards of the Covenant—to the nation to determine how greatly out of line she really is.

The test reveals that the nation is so far from being plumb that she can no longer be allowed to stand. The Lord will not "again pass by them" (vs. 8), that is, he will not again relent as he did before. The whole structure is so bad that it will have to come down. The local high places, the sanctuaries which had been turned into places of apostasy, will become "desolate" (vs. 9). And the whole "house of Jeroboam" will be destroyed by the sword. The Assyrian armies will accomplish that.

Historical Interlude: Amaziah and Amos (7:10-17)

This section, as noted above, interrupts the series of visions in chapters 7-9, but it throws considerable and welcome light on the prophetic inspiration of Amos and on the treatment he received at the hands of his compatriots in Israel.

Amaziah's Message to Jeroboam (7:10-11)

Amaziah was the chief priest of Bethel and, as such, one of the officials of the kingdom. He, with the king and his council and officers, together with the property holders, formed the group so severely rebuked by Amos. In these verses it is evident that the sting of the prophet's oracles was having its effect. The priest used the term "conspire" in informing the king of the preaching of Amos. Actually, of course, the charge was not true, but in desperation Amaziah had virtually no other choice than to make it, for he had no effective answer to the pronouncements of the prophet. Hence he tried to turn his judgments into pronouncements of conspiracy and treason. The words attributed to Amos by Amaziah were true only in part, for the former had never threatened the life of the king personally. He had spoken (vs. 9) against the house of Jeroboam, but that represented the whole ruling class without reference to a specific person. The charge of the priest must have been couched in personal terms to arouse the king to summary action against the unwelcome intruder from Tekoa. This is a classic illustration of taking ideas out of context and giving them an altogether different meaning by slight subtraction or addition of words. Surely the land *as it was* could not "bear all his words," but it was possible to make the land *as it ought to have been* by conforming, in repentance, to the Covenant of the Lord.

Amaziah's Warning to Amos (7:12-13)

Amaziah's advice to Amos was, if anything, more presumptuous and humiliating than his report to the king had been misleading. The term "seer" by this time may have been a derogatory expression meaning something like our "visionary" or "stargazer" (see Micah 3:7). Earlier it had been a perfectly good word describing one to whom visions were given by the Lord (see, for example, II Sam. 24:11; II Chron. 9:29; 19:2). In any case, Amos received a less than polite invitation to leave the country and go home "to the land of Judah" (vs. 12). There he could have free range to express his thoughts about Israel; in fact, the people of Judah would be happy to hear what he had to say about their rival to the north. They might even pay him for his efforts. Seers did receive pay for their advice on occasion (I Sam. 9:7-8), and some prophets gave oracles for hire (Micah 3:5, 11). The true prophet, however, was not interested in compensation but preached solely for the good of the nation.

Along with the opprobrium heaped upon the prophet went the more or less solemn warning never again to cross theological swords with the ordained religious leaders of Bethel. Bethel was the official royal sanctuary of Jeroboam, "a temple of the kingdom" (vs. 13). The fashionable sanctuary of Bethel must never again be disturbed by such harsh and uncouth words, nor its sacred precincts and ceremonies desecrated by the lips of the hillbilly of the desert!

Amos' Reply to Amaziah (7:14-17)

The words of Amaziah were perhaps calculated to trap Amos into issuing a devastating blast against the king. If so, they failed of their objective. The response of Amos is a restatement of his call, a reiteration of the Lord's judgment upon the land, and a scathing prophecy against the priest himself. In reply to the accusation directed at him by Amaziah, Amos disavows any connection with the professional prophets. He says he had not been a prophet by descent or profession before the moment when the Lord called him from his occupation as "herdsman, and a dresser of sycamore trees" (vss. 14-15). The Lord *took* him from his normal position and commanded him to go and prophesy. There was no thought of earning bread, no promise of special consideration, and no indication of a great career.

Having cleared up the matter of his call and credentials, the prophet immediately launched into a restatement of the word of the Lord to Israel. He had been sent to give the word of the Lord to the very one who now ordered him out of town with the admonition not to "prophesy against Israel" or "preach against the house of Isaac" (vs. 16). The prophecy against Amaziah is presented in the same vein as the earlier ones, that is, against the background of judgment in the form of invasion and subsequent captivity. The still youthful wife of Amaziah will be forced into harlotry with foreign soldiers right in the city, a shocking thing even to contemplate (vs. 17; see Isa. 13:16; Zech. 14:2). Their sons and daughters will fall victim to the sword, and the land given to the priest for his support will be "parceled out by line." The end of the matter will come when he himself will be taken captive, transported, and die "in an unclean land." The reference, of course, is to a foreign land; all lands outside Israel were regarded as unclean. Finally there came the solemn reassertion that Israel must go into exile, repeated verbatim from the words which Amaziah had put into the mouth of the prophet (vs. 11). It was not a very successful encounter for the priest of Bethel.

The Basket of Summer Fruit (8:1-3)

The time for judgment is ripe—that is the message of the vision of a basket of "summer fruit" (8:1). The connection between "summer fruit" and "the end" (vs. 2) is more vivid in the original (where there is a play on the two words) than in translation. The sight of summer fruit, well ripened, always does mean that the end of the growing season is at hand. The symbol is used here to drive home the lesson that the end of the season for repentance has come for Israel. God's determination never again to relent is repeated (as in 7:8), and, in fact, is emphasized by the nature of the vision which stressed "the end."

There follows a description of what the end will mean. The joyful festivals in which the people and priests delight will cease, the accompanying songs will be turned into howling, and wailing and despair will replace the present display of easy confidence (vs. 3). "That day" again refers to the Day of the Lord heralded in 5:18-20, the Day of judgment which will fall upon them rather than upon their enemies as they had expected. The horror of that Day is reflected by the following passage: "the dead bodies shall be many; in every place they shall be cast out in silence." The survivors will be compelled to dispose of the heaped-up bodies in silence and despair (see 6:10).

Judgments for Sin (8:4-14)

Here we have a series of judgments which repeat many of the charges leveled against Israel in the previous oracles.

No Time for the Lord (8:4-6)

The first complaint of Amos is against those who put their unfortunate brethren under constant and deliberate pressure, in order to gain more for themselves. They trampled "upon the needy." (Another possible meaning is that they "snared" the needy or "panted" after them in the hope of getting what they wanted from them.) In so doing they threatened to reduce the poorer classes of people to slavery and bring them to an end. Such treatment expressed itself in many forms: in divesting of their property those who could not help themselves, as in the case of Naboth (I Kings 21); foreclosure (Isa. 5:8); forced labor without just compensation (Jer. 22:13); and even slavery. The accusations here center for the most part about commercial dealings. The spirit of commercialism had rooted itself so deeply into the life of the nation that its devotees could hardly wait for holy days to pass, in order that they might ply their lucrative trade. The overwhelming influence of that spirit with its desire for gain may be seen in the second half of verse 5. These rapacious merchants had acquired the habit of using short measures and light weights when selling products to their customers and of the reverse process when buying goods. Manipulation of scales or weights was an abomination to the Lord (Lev. 19:36; Deut. 25: 13, 15; Prov. 11:1; Micah 6:11).

One phase of the transaction denounced in verse 6 has been discussed in connection with 2:6. There the selling phase was emphasized; here it is the buying side of the deal. This is more than dealing in human commodities, which would be bad enough for a supposedly covenanted people. It is related to the whole process of deception and false dealing. These commercial opportunists knew how to maneuver helpless people into a corner where they were forced to sell themselves into slavery for a price just large enough to make the transaction legal.

An additional charge, that they "sell the refuse of the wheat," is rather difficult to interpret in its present position. It may be a piece of "floating" Amos tradition, which was attached to this oracle because of its commercial vocabulary. It means either that in their greed the merchants sell what ought to be discarded, or that they mix in with the good grain what ought to have gone for animal feed, thus deriving a higher price.

Judgment (8:7-10)

Like 4:2 and 6:8, this oracle is in the form of an oath sworn by the Lord. The first one was sworn by the holiness of the Lord, the second by the Lord himself, and this one "by the pride of Jacob" (vs. 7), which may be a substitute expression for the Lord himself (see I Sam. 15: 29 where the Lord is referred to as the "Glory" or "Eminence" of Israel). The fact that he "will never forget any of their deeds" emphasizes God's involvement with those he has created. The evil which the powerful have contrived against the weak concerns not only human relationships but also the divine-human relationship, and is an evil committed against God as well as against man.

Since there was no disposition on the part of those who did the wrong to repent and make amends, judgment must follow. That judgment will affect everything, even nature (vs. 8). The wickedness of the people is so terrible that the very soil beneath their feet will tremble and shake; it will rebel against them, so that every inhabitant will mourn when it begins to quake. The comparison to an abnormal inundation of the Nile is suggestive, for it recalls the plagues described in Exodus, which were in themselves a judgment upon the recalcitrant Egyptians. The land will "rise like the Nile, and be tossed about and sink again."

Along with the upheavals of nature will go celestial phenomena which also conspire against evil (vs. 9). There was an eclipse of the sun on June 15, 763 B.C., visible in Palestine, and therefore recent enough to be remembered by the hearers of Amos. Obviously such an event is presupposed by his reference to the sun going down "at noon" and the darkening of the earth "in broad daylight." "That day," to which the prophet points, was to be one of stern reckoning, when *Israel's* world would literally come to an end. The refusal of the nation to repent and to accept the word of the Lord was responsible for the catastrophe, and though Amos painted a moving picture of the event in terms of natural phenomena, he was not predicting a universal disaster.

When the enemy strikes it will be "a bitter day" indeed (vs. 10). The "feasts" or "festivals" of joy, such as those of the harvest and vintage, will be turned into weeping, that is, into times of sorrow and despair. Lyrics will become dirges. There will be no blessings in the land, only suffering, privation, and death. With the lamentation will go the customary signs of sackcloth and shaved head. The attendant mourning will be like that for an only son (see Jer. 6:26; Zech. 12:10). The God of blessing thus becomes the God of judgment and desolation, and the Day of the Lord brings sorrow rather than joy, adversity rather than prosperity, destruction for the nation rather than for her foes.

Famine of the Word of God (8:11-12)

The expression, "the days are coming" (vs. 11), is another way of referring to the Day of the Lord's judgment when the dire consequences will naturally send the people inquiring after his word. But it will be a day of famine of the word of the Lord (see I Sam. 3:1) as well as famine of bread and water. The people had not realized that man cannot live by bread alone but "by everything that proceeds out of the mouth of the LORD" (Deut. 8:3). In that day people will run from place to place in search of a prophet who will declare to them the "words of the LORD," only to discover that there is available neither spokesman nor word.

Their search for the word of the Lord reaches to the very limits of the land itself—"from sea to sea," that is, from the Dead Sea, the southernmost border of Israel, to the Mediterranean, its western border (vs. 12). In their search they will "wander" about (literally "stagger") exhausted and uncertain because they are ignorant of the word. The more they search the more confused will they become, as the term "run to and fro" suggests. How often God had spoken to them before, but they refused to listen; now their constant and stubborn resistance has so hardened them that they are unable to discern his presence and hence they will not find him in their distress.

Denunciation of Syncretism (8:13-14)

This difficult passage is apparently an addition to the original prophecy of Amos, at least in its present form, doubtless located here because of the reference to "thirst," which occurs in verses

11 and 13, and to famine which is always accompanied by a shortage of water. The passage itself is introduced by the phrase "in that day" which is common in the oracles of judgment. When "that day" arrives it will sweep away not only the mature, the fathers and mothers, but also the "fair virgins" and the equally fair "young men," who are the hope of the future.

"Those who swear by Ashimah of Samaria" (vs. 14) are probably adherents of a religion which grew up in the region after the fall of the Northern Kingdom, when other peoples were brought into the land by the Assyrians (II Kings 17:24-34). Despite later purges and destructions of Bethel, the cult appears to have survived there. Correspondence between a colony of Jews at Elephantine in Egypt and the Jews of Bethel has been discovered, dating from the fifth century B.C. At Elephantine there was a deity called "Eshem-bethel" which has here been altered to "Eshem-Samaria" (meaning "the name of Samaria"). What is meant by "thy god . . . O Dan" and "the way of Beer-sheba" is not clear at present, but likely underlying them is a similar alteration of names. The judgment pronounced upon these later apostates is the same as that threatened against the corrupters of Israel; these "shall fall, and never rise again."

The Vision at the Altar (9:1-6)

At the beginning of chapter 9 comes the fifth vision of Amos, the series having been interrupted, first by the exchange between him and Amaziah (7:10-17), and second by the pronouncements of judgment because of the persistence of the people in their breach of the Covenant.

No Escape (9:1-4)

The prophet speaks of looking on as the assembly of Israel had gathered at the sacred shrine of the kingdom for worship. There he sees the Lord standing beside the altar and commanding that the building be struck down and the worshipers destroyed. The one to whom he gives command is not specified, but is in all probability a member of the intimate council of the Lord who is designated to carry out his orders. He is to smite the "capitals" (vs. 1), apparently either the architrave or the ornamental caps of the pillars. The thresholds would naturally shake when the capitals and architrave were struck down. The whole concept developed here may rest on the account of Samson's overthrow of the Philistines in the temple of Dagon (Judges 16:28-30) or on Jehu's destruction of the adherents of Baal (II Kings 10:18-27). Those who remain or escape death in such a destruction will be slain with the sword.

The warnings, "though they dig into Sheol . . . though they climb up to heaven" (vs. 2), carry forward the idea that there will be no escape for the sinner. Even though he flees to places beyond the reach of man, he cannot get away from God (see 5:18-19). His hand will "take them" and "bring them down." There can be no hiding from God, for he knows even the most obscure recesses of the caves of Mount Carmel and has at his command the serpent (the monster) of the sea. Even captivity in the land of an enemy country will offer no security, for the Lord has set his "eyes upon them for evil and not for good" (vs. 4).

The Greatness of the Lord (9:5-6)

Such a dire threat requires substantiation of the greatness and omnipotence of the Lord, and to that subject Amos now turns. The God whose servant he is, is the Creator who knows the ends of the earth. He is the one who speaks and it is done. "He . . . touches the earth and it melts" (vs. 5). He is the Creator of the earth, which is alive and breathes, and rises in the upheaval of earthquake like the yearly flood of the Nile, and then sinks back again in rest until the next breath. He has erected the gigantic structure of the heavens, "his upper chambers" (vs. 6). The pattern of thought here is that of Genesis 1:6-8. The sky was believed to be a solid firmament in the form of a "vault" or arch, whose bases rested on the earth. The realm above was the place where God dwelt, and the heavenly bodies were like lanterns hung from the rafters of the firmament, or carried across the sky as the sun, moon, and planets. God is the Author and Provider of the rains which fertilized the land (see 5:8). As guardian of that which made life possible he is the preserver of his creation.

Hope for Israel (9:7-15)

These final verses of the book are frequently denied to Amos, on the ground that up to this point his oracles and visions have been uncompromising in their insistence upon the total destruction of the nation, without hope for survival. Also, it has been said that the poetry here is less vigorous and elemental, and does not begin to match that of the genuine prophecies. While the Book of Amos was certainly not the composition of the prophet himself, but of an editor, and while doubtless some materials that are not actually the work of Amos are present, it does not do justice to the prophet to rule out as unauthentic all messages of hope. There are elsewhere in the book undisputed references to his own plea for mercy (for example, 7:2-3, 5-6), and the very fact that he was sent to proclaim God's judgment is in itself not a pronouncement of unqualified doom but the expression of a desire that the nation repent. Also the fact that he offers suggestions concerning demands of God for maintenance of the Covenant implies strongly that he had some measure of hope that there might actually be repentance (for example, 5:4, 6, 14, 24).

The Lord of the Nations (9:7)

The best commentary on verse 7 is chapters 1 and 2 of Amos. There he already hints at the conception here voiced. The Lord is there represented as judging the nations for their excesses, just as he is going to judge Israel for hers. He is the Lord of the nations as well as of Israel. But Israel had always proudly asserted her special relationship to him in her peculiar interpretation of the doctrine of election (see on 3:2). With one fell sweep Amos brushes aside that misconception of special privilege and asserts that Israel is on the same basis as other nations. The Lord had brought Israel out of Egypt, but the Lord had also brought the Philistines from Caphtor and the Syrians from Kir. To the Lord, Israel was just like the Ethiopians, the traditional slave nation. The full consequences of Amos' words have not yet been fully grasped, but they are as applicable today as then. The God of Amos is the sovereign God of all the earth and all the nations are his servants, for good or for ill (see also Acts 10:34-35; Rom. 2:11; Eph. 6:9; James 2:1).

The Universal Standards of Justice (9:8-10)

The Lord did, in fact, bring the Israelites up out of the land of Egypt, and he gave them a land of their own, but that did not confer on them the privilege of doing as they pleased. As God specifically said earlier through Amos (3:2), deliverance and superior perception of his will, together with the whole body of revelation given through lawgiver and prophet, put them in a unique posi-

tion of *obedience and service*. Therefore, "the eyes of the Lord
GOD are upon the sinful kingdom" (vs. 8). The people did not
serve him; they sinned even above others who had less understanding of his will. God does not overlook the wrongs of others;
how can he overlook those of a people who know better?

But he "will not utterly destroy the house of Jacob." That is
the foundation of the idea of the Remnant, so prominent in Isaiah, and may itself be based in part on the earlier tradition current in the Elijah stories (I Kings 19:18). Here, then, we have
actually a qualification of what earlier seemed to be a pronouncement of unqualified destruction. Amos was an uncompromising advocate of God's justice, but that justice would not permit discrimination against the ones in the nation who had been
faithful to the Covenant.

Verses 9-10 are a further application of the same principle.
Amos does not retract anything he has said; he simply works it
out further. The nation must go into exile among the nations.
That great new experience will function as a sieve wherein Israel
will be shaken to and fro as grain is shaken. The defective ker-
nels will fall through to the ground but the good grain will remain. Not one good grain ("pebble") will "fall upon the earth."
What that means is that "the sinners of my people shall die by
the sword," particularly those who say, "Evil shall not overtake
or meet us." These were the ones who thought their election con-
ferred an absolute security upon them as the people of God.

Restoration for Redeemed Israel (9:11-15)

These verses are often viewed as the epilogue of the Book of
Amos, coming from a date later than the original prophecy. Even
those who allow the authenticity of the preceding section generally ascribe these verses to a later period. The arguments for a
later date, however, are not convincing. The prophet begins by
referring to "that day" (see 8:9, 13); that is, the day when judgment and the refining process have done their work. There is a
real sense in which the Day of judgment is also the Day of salvation; when judgment is finished there will be salvation. That is
the conclusion to which the prophet comes. He was not alone in
that belief; his younger contemporary and fellow countryman,
Isaiah, had almost the same view, for after a scathing condemnation of Judah, he proclaimed not only the doctrine of the Remnant but also that of a Messiah. It is not too much to believe that

Amos had dreams of a reunion of the two parts of the divided house of Israel, to which he refers as "the booth of David that is fallen" (vs. 11). That clause can just as well mean the breach of the kingdom, which Isaiah so laments (Isa. 7:17), as the fallen kingdom of Judah. Later prophets, even long after the fall of the Northern Kingdom, looked for a restoration and reunion of the two kingdoms (see, for example, Ezek. 23; 37:15-28). In any event, the prophet looks forward to a rebuilding of the Davidic kingdom, although there is no mention of a Messianic king. The reference to Edom is to be expected, because there always was strong feeling between Israel and Edom. The latter had been severely dealt with by Amaziah of Judah twenty-five years or more before the appearance of Amos (II Kings 14:7). Later on Edom took advantage of Judah and made forays into the country (II Chron. 28:17), and still later, after the Captivity, occupied some of Judah's territory (Ezek. 35:14-15). But Amos does not stop with Edom; he visualizes a time when "all the nations" which are called by the name of the Lord shall once again be restored as they were under the Davidic empire, so that it will become "as in the days of old" (vss. 11-12). This passage is quoted by James in his address to the Apostolic Council in Acts 15:16-17.

The final oracle begins, "Behold, the days are coming," as did the ones in 4:2 and 8:11. Here, however, the reference is to the glorious and happy days after the judgment and restoration. This is a grand poetic piece, describing the response of nature in blessing and support of the people who have been purged and purified and brought back to the ancestral heritage. So fruitful will the land be, so rich and rapid its productivity, that "the plowman shall overtake the reaper" and "the treader" of the wine press "him who sows the seed" (vs. 13). In the coming days the people shall enjoy the fruit of the vine, a symbol of peace and prosperity (see Isa. 37:30; Jer. 32:15; Ezek. 28:26; Lev. 26:5). All this will take place when the Lord restores the captivity of his people ("the fortunes of my people"). Then shall they rebuild the ruined cities and dwell in them and enjoy the fruit of planted vineyard and garden. The restoration, moreover, will be permanent, for they shall be planted upon their land and never again be uprooted. That is the word of the Lord to his people—but to a people who are refined by the fires of exile, who are penitent, and who remain faithful to his Covenant of blessings and grace.

THE BOOK OF

OBADIAH

INTRODUCTION

Authorship and Date

There can be no reasonable doubt that the deliverer of the prophecy in this book was a man by the name of Obadiah ("the one who serves the Lord"). We have no means of knowing many details of his life. From a study of his prophecy it is certain that he was an ardent Judean, a devoted servant of the Lord, a student of history, and an enemy of Edom.

It is generally believed that the Book of Obadiah is composed of at least two distinct parts, 1-14 and 15b; 15a and 16-21. Some interpreters see in each of these larger parts two or more divisions, or perhaps editorial expansions. But it is not necessary to go that far. That there are two phases in the prophecy may be regarded as certain. The first phase appears to deal with a situation which is quite recent and which has profoundly affected the thought and attitude of the prophet. The second phase may represent a slightly later situation when Edom was beginning to move into southern Judah, in the wake of pressure from Arab invaders which must have begun before the end of the sixth century B.C.

One of the most important events in the whole history of Israel (Judah) was the fall of Jerusalem in 587 B.C. The Edomites evidently had a hand in that catastrophe (Ps. 137:7) and received some of the spoil, together with portions of Judean territory (Joel 3:2-3). Something of the arrogant attitude of the Edomites is reflected in Lamentations 4:21-22. The whole tenor of the first half of Obadiah makes it quite apparent that the event was not far removed from the time of its composition. The second portion seems to be the product of further reflection on that event and the application of the concept of the Day of the Lord (vs. 15a) to Edom, possibly in the light of the Arab pressure noted above. Those observations would place the origin of part of Obadiah's prophecy soon after the fall of Jerusalem and the other part sometime later in that century. Absolute dates are impossible.

Composition

The composition of the little book has already been hinted at. There was, in all probability, a body (or book) of oracles against foreign nations which was drawn upon by more than one prophet. There is a series of such prophecies in Amos (1-2), Isaiah (13-23), Jeremiah (46-51), Ezekiel (25-32). In speaking out against foreign nations the prophets must have utilized some of the oracular material at hand. Obadiah is an excellent example of that process, for there are clear and unmistakable similarities between his observations and those in Jeremiah (for example, Obad. 1b and Jer. 49:14; Obad. 2 and Jer. 49:15; Obad. 3 and Jer. 49:16; Obad. 4 and Jer. 49:16; Obad. 5 and Jer. 49:9). That there is a correspondence between these passages can hardly be denied, but whether there was direct literary borrowing by Obadiah is another question. Both oracles may have drawn upon a common source, though that cannot be proved. Such borrowing does not detract from the vigor and force with which the author invested and applied his materials. It only indicates the complexity of the problem of literary relationships.

Purpose and Message

The purpose of Obadiah is closely related to his permanent message. In a sense, our book is a message of hope for Judah (17-21). It offers reassurance to a downtrodden and defeated people in captivity and poverty. Despite the outwardly hopeless present there is in store for them a better day.

The hope for that better day rests on the prophet's belief that there is no escape from judgment even for proud, isolated, and naturally protected Edom. The sin of the Edomites—their failure to uphold the Covenant of brotherhood—will find them out (2-4). Along with the judgment upon Edom for its repulsive acts toward Judah in her day of trouble, there is a broader lesson, that of a national justice operative in the world. Nations, at whatever juncture in history, must answer before the bar of history for their pride or evil acts. We sometimes think of Obadiah as a prophet of vengeance, but that is unfair. He is rather a firm advocate of the idea of the vindication of the Lord and of his promises to his people as the principle of justice is applied in the society of nations. And justice does not conflict with love; it is love's vindication on a national and social level.

Perhaps the greatest message of Obadiah as the book now stands is the unequivocal assertion that "the kingdom shall be the LORD's." The author of the Book of Revelation based his message on just such a faith in the ultimate victory of Christ when he heard the loud voices from heaven in response to the trumpet blast of the seventh angel, "The kingdom of the world has become the kingdom of our Lord and of his Christ, and he shall reign for ever and ever" (Rev. 11:15).

OUTLINE

COMMENTARY

AN ORACLE ON THE DOOM OF EDOM
Obadiah 1-9

The first nine verses of Obadiah comprise the basic portion of the book. They present the prophet's prediction of the utter destruction of Edom. Her mountain situation will afford no protection nor will her traditionally wise men be able to save her.

The Superscription (1a)

There are twelve other persons by the name of Obadiah in the Old Testament, but there is no reason to connect this prophet with any one of them. We know nothing at all about Obadiah the prophet except what may be gleaned from his prophecy.

An Accounting for Edom (1b-4)

Oracles against Edom, the descendants of Jacob's twin brother Esau, abound in the prophets (Isa. 34:5-15; Ezek. 35; Jer. 49: 7-22; Amos 1:11-12; Mal. 1:2-5), and in other literature there are derogatory references (for example, Lam. 4:21b; Ps. 137: 7). Much of this oracle is similar to Jeremiah 49, and Obadiah may be simply reporting or applying earlier oracles against the proverbial foe of Israel. "We have heard tidings from the LORD" (vs. 1) may be no more than an appeal to earlier revelation, like Joel's appeal to Obadiah 17 (Joel 2: 32b). This does not detract from the vision of Obadiah; it rather strengthens it because it demonstrates the correctness of earlier visions and views.

The vision is from the Lord concerning Edom. There is no exhortation to Judah because Judah is not in a position to take action; the little nation was probably no longer in existence at the time. The word "tidings" (report) points to rumors of an uprising against Edom, for which the Lord was responsible; the prophet visualizes a messenger as having been sent from the Lord to stir up the nations against Edom.

What the Lord had to say about Edom begins with verse 2. The Hebrew here indicates that the Lord has already determined to humiliate Edom, and thus it is as good as done, though it has not actually taken place. That such is the case may be seen from the fact that Edom is still enjoying security in its mountain fortress. The report which the prophet heard from the Lord was that very soon Edom will be in the same position as Judah is now— small, and impotent on the international scene. To be "utterly despised" means not so much to be held in contempt, as to be so small and weak as to afford no serious threat of resistance to any hostile power. Jeremiah 49:15 brings that out clearly and forcefully.

Hitherto Edom has relied on its mountain fastnesses to protect it. Whenever outsiders threatened it, Edom withdrew into the well-nigh inaccessible places around the center of Petra (vs. 3; see margin "Sela," which is "rock"). Obviously the leaders boasted of the strength of their position (see Ezek. 35:13), as verse 3 shows, but this time their proud hearts will be deceived by the very things upon which they counted. The mountains around Petra are high and precipitous, the passageways narrow and dark, offering excellent shelter and hiding places from the enemy. The expression "whose dwelling is high" reflects the location of the city, surrounded by mountains from three to five thousand feet high, and most difficult of access. In an invasion, the inhabitants could well think, "Who will [or can] bring me down to the ground?" But though they soar aloft to the mountain fortress like an eagle (vs. 4; see Job 39:27-28) and set their "nest" (their dwellings) "among the stars," they will not be able to escape the hand of the Lord (see Jer. 49:16 for a slightly different version of the same expression). No nation, no matter how strong or impregnable, can escape the judgment of God.

Total Destruction for Edom (5-9)

Verse 5 is paralleled in Jeremiah 49:9. The ejaculation of Obadiah, "How you have been destroyed!" points to the utter destruction and desolation of Edom. Even thieves would not produce such havoc. They would take only enough for their meals and leave something for the owners of the property. Even grape gatherers would leave some gleanings, perhaps for the poor of the land. But the prophet sees nothing left for Edom but the bare land and barren rocks. Proud Edom will thus be brought low and all one can do is raise a lamentation for land and people. The prophet himself is led to exclaim in astonishment, "How Esau has been pillaged, his treasures sought out!" (vs. 6; see Jer. 49:10). The terms "allies," "confederates," and "trusted friends" in verse 7 reflect the alliances between Edom and the Arab tribes before the fifth century B.C. These "allies" have now not only deserted Edom but have actually taken it by surprise and treachery. "Confederates" are those who are in formal relationship (the word for "treaty" or "covenant" is used) and "trusted friends" are, literally, "those who eat your bread"—a symbol of the closest kind of fellowship. These very close associates have now turned against Edom, with the result that the people of Edom are bewildered. Forsaken by those who were their treaty-bound allies, and pushed out of their fortresses, they are utterly helpless.

The celebrated wisdom of Edom will also be the victim of destruction "on that day" (vs. 8); that is, at the time when the Lord will act against this nation, rather than the ultimate Day of Judgment. Edom was known for its wise men; Eliphaz, one of the friends of Job, was a Temanite. Jeremiah (49:7) also refers to the wisdom of Teman. In Job 15:18-19, Eliphaz refers to the tradition of the wise men current in his land. In any case, wisdom and understanding will perish with the land and its inhabitants.

On the "dismay" of the mighty men of Teman (vs. 9), see Jeremiah 49:22. Teman was an important town of Edom, probably modern Tawilan, a few miles to the east of the old city of Petra. The mighty men will be so terrorized that the rest of the Edomites may be put to the sword. Taken by and large, this is a heavy penalty to pay for the deeds of which the nation was guilty. What those deeds were we shall see below, but certainly the relentless forces of history were making themselves felt against the people whom Obadiah called boastful and proud. Beneath the apparently ruthless action of the Lord is the conception of vindication of the Lord and his people. For other nations to prevail forever would have meant the utter failure of the Lord and his Covenant.

THE REASONS FOR EDOM'S DESTRUCTION

Obadiah 10-14

Among the reasons cited by the prophet for the coming destruction is Edom's guilt with reference to Jacob—it is "for the violence done to your brother Jacob" (vs. 10). From their natal day Jacob and Esau carried on a feud (see Gen. 25:23-34), which continued with few exceptions throughout the history of their descendants. The history of Israel is full of instances of Edom's opposition (Num. 20:14-21; Judges 11:17; II Chron. 21:8-10: 28:17; Ezek. 25:12; Ps. 137:7) and of Israel's retaliation (I Sam. 14:47; II Sam. 8:13-14; I Kings 11:14-16; II Kings 14:7-10; II Chron. 25:11-13). But at the same time Israel was exhorted by the Deuteronomist to let Edom alone (Deut. 2:4-5) and never to abhor an Edomite, because he was his brother (Deut. 23:7). The crucial word in Obadiah and in the second reference in Deuteronomy is "brother." Amos (1:11) also speaks of Esau's pursuing his brother with the sword. Here the clear emphasis is upon the violation of the Covenant of brotherhood which, as just observed, had a long history. The straw that broke the camel's back, however, was the attitude of Edom after the fall of Jerusalem, to which it was evidently a party. It received some of the territory belonging to Judah, and somewhat later, because of external pressure, was compelled to move into what was previously southern Judah. In other words, there was encroachment upon Judah and seizure of her land. For that act Edom was to be "cut off for ever"—a prophecy fulfilled several centuries later when Judas Maccabaeus defeated and plundered the Edomites (I Macc. 5:3) and John Hyrcanus completely subjugated them a half century later.

Obadiah accuses Edom of standing "aloof" (vs. 11; literally, "on the other side" or "in opposition") when Judah was in dire need. Instead of acting like a brother, Edom actually cast its lot with the enemy and destroyer. The statement, "you were like one of them," voices the prophet's bitter complaint against Edom's conspiracy with the Chaldeans in the moment of Judah's catastrophe.

The depth of feeling on the part of the prophet is not conveyed adequately in the translation of the next three verses (12-14). Obadiah speaks as if the whole thing were taking place right before his very eyes. Each line begins with "you should not" (literally, "you must not"), just as if he were talking directly to the guilty nation at the moment. He says in effect: "You must not look (with approbation) upon the day of your brother, in the day of his misfortune" (vs. 12), which they apparently did. "You must not rejoice over the people of Judah in the day of their ruin" (vs. 12; see Lam. 4:21-22). "You must not boast in the day of distress" (vs. 12). "You must not enter the gate of my people in the day of their calamity" (vs. 13). "You must not look (with approval) upon his disaster in the day of his calamity" (vs. 13). "You must not loot his goods in the day of his calamity" (vs. 13; see Joel 3:2-3). "You must not stand at the parting of the ways to cut off his fugitives" (vs. 14), which points not only to the cutting off of ways of retreat, but the capture and return of escapees to their pursuers. "You must not hand over his survivors in the day of distress" (vs. 14). Such acts on the part of Jacob's brother cannot be condoned.

THE DAY OF JUDGMENT
Obadiah 15-16

In the general judgment which is approaching, all nations will be involved (see also Joel 3:2; Zeph. 1; Amos 5:18-20). That concept is the basis for Obadiah's application of the principle of judgment to Edom in the last part of verse 15, which may be the conclusion of the preceding section. As such it brings out quite effectively the principle of retribution to be applied to that nation: "As you have done, it shall be done to you" (vs. 15; see Mark 4:24). The above accusations will thus become the basis upon which Edom will be judged in the day of the Lord's judgment of all nations (see Isa. 3:11; Hab. 2:8; Rev. 18:6).

If what has just been said is the proper interpretation and division of verses, then the first part of verse 15 is an introduction to verse 16 which, in all probability, refers to Judah. The great day of judgment for all nations has affected Judah as it will Edom. Judah has, in fact, already begun to experience the judgment of the Day of the Lord—"you have drunk upon my holy mountain" (vs. 16). She has suffered for her sins. Now it is the turn of others to fall under the righteous scrutiny of the Lord. They, too, "shall drink, and stagger." (For the figure see Isa. 51:17, 22; Jer. 25:15-16; Ezek. 23:32-34; John 18:11; Rev. 14:10, 15-19.) They will "be as though they had not been."

JACOB'S RULE OVER ESAU
Obadiah 17-18

The first part of verse 17 is quoted by Joel (2:32), and the idea of a remnant's escaping goes back at least to Isaiah 10:21-22. The hope of deliverance, which is an old conception of the prophets, had been realized to some extent by the time of Obadiah. Not all Judah was destroyed by the Chaldean invasion; some of the people were left in the land, some fled to Egypt, and some were taken into captivity. From the captives came the re-

turnees who later re-established the religious institutions of the
land in the time of Haggai and Zechariah. Judgment had come
upon Judah but some had escaped. The righteousness of God
was at work in the land, and now was making itself felt elsewhere. Mount Zion shall now be holy; that is, it will be no more
desecrated by the nations (see Joel 3:17). "The house of Jacob"
(Judah) will regain its old possessions, return to the land, take
up residence there, and assume possession of its fields and
lands.

Verse 18 clearly deals with the future, since it looks forward
to the time when the two kingdoms—the house of Jacob (Judah)
and the house of Joseph (Israel)—will be reunited in restoration
(Isa. 11:13; Jer. 3:18; Ezek. 37:16-17; Hosea 3:5; Zech. 10:6).
Then will take place the defeat and destruction of their enemies.
(For the symbol of fire and stubble, see Isaiah 10:17; Zechariah
12:6; Malachi 4:1.) Because of Esau's (Edom's) dastardly deeds
against his brother (vss. 12-14), his house will be without sur-
vivor. The words, "for the LORD has spoken," are like a signature
of the Eternal, establishing the validity of the prophecy.

THE APPORTIONING OF THE NATIONS
TO JUDAH
Obadiah 19-20

It will be recalled that after the fall of Jerusalem in 587 B.C.,
some of the territory of Judah was apportioned to Edom. After
the coming judgment the tables will be turned, and to Judah will
be apportioned "Mount Esau" (vs. 19). The Edomites living in
the extreme southern part of Judah (the Negeb) will be dispos-
sessed by a segment of the returning Judeans. Others of the re-
turnees will go to "the Shephelah the land of the Philistines,"
that is, the foothills west of Bethlehem (see Zeph. 2:5-7). Some
will enter and take possession of "the land of Ephraim and the
land of Samaria," that is, the hill country known as the highlands
of Ephraim, extending from Bethel to the plain of Jezreel. In the
wake of that movement the Benjamites would naturally be
squeezed out, but in compensation they will be given Gilead, the
area in Transjordan between the Jabbok and Yarmuk Rivers.
On the other hand, for the reference to Benjamin here the original may have read "the sons of Ammon," in which case verse

19b would read, "they shall possess the territory of Ephraim and the territory of Samaria and the Ammonites with Gilead."

Verse 20 is difficult but certainly recapitulates what has been said in the preceding verses about the return of the house of Jacob and the house of Joseph. The emended text from which the translation of the Revised Standard Version is derived says that the exiles of the Northern Kingdom at Halah, where they were settled by the Assyrians after the conquest of Samaria (II Kings 17:6), "shall possess Phoenicia as far as Zarephath," a small village on the Mediterranean coast between Tyre and Sidon (I Kings 17:9; Luke 4:26). Halah was a district in north Mesopotamia, actually unknown, but probably to the east of Carchemish. "The exiles of Jerusalem who are in Sepharad shall possess the cities of the Negeb." Sepharad was probably Sardis in Asia Minor, where a text has been found indicating the presence of Jews in the time of Artaxerxes I (465-424 B.C.). Apart from this, the significance of the reference escapes us.

THE LORD'S KINGDOM
Obadiah 21

Deliverers shall ascend Mount Zion to govern Mount Esau— the holy mount versus the mount of profanation. The idea of the "deliverer" or "savior" is apparently based on the judges (see Judges 2:16), who are also referred to as deliverers, and may reflect the attitude toward certain personalities of the late postexilic period who had a hand in the restoration of Judah. On the other hand, it may actually be a prophecy of things to come, on the basis of the conception of "the prince" in Ezekiel (see Ezek. 45-46). In any event, the prophet visualizes rulers or deliverers bringing Mount Esau into subjection so that it will not again exercise its inconsiderate influence over Israel.

Through the judgment and vindication of his people, together with the subjection of their enemies, God will establish his dominion. This realization of the nation's hope through the righteousness of God points forward to the New Testament. In the final analysis the Lord is God, and his Kingdom not only will come but must come. God has the last word, and his righteousness will prevail in the restoration of his people and in the judgment of the nations. That is the faith of Obadiah.

THE BOOK OF

JONAH

INTRODUCTION

Authorship and Date

We can be certain that Jonah is not the author of the book
that bears his name. So much is evident from the fact that the
book is composed almost entirely in the third person, with the
quotation of supposed words of the prophet occurring only spo-
radically. But who the author was we do not know. We do know
that he was a pious Jew who had caught the true spirit of Israelite religion, especially as it was revealed in the prophets.

Just when the Book of Jonah was written is another unsolved
enigma. It cannot be earlier than the reference to the prophet
Jonah ben Amittai in II Kings 14:25, in the period of Jeroboam
II (786-746 B.C.). Nor can it be later than about 200 B.C., for
Ecclesiasticus, in the Apocrypha, written about that time, refers
to "the twelve prophets" (Ecclus. 49:10), and the experience of
Jonah is used for illustrative purposes in another book of that
time (Tobit 14:4, 8).

The date of the book must be sought in the historical development of Hebrew thought and life. While the prophets before the
Exile were concerned about the nations of the world and brought
them under the judgment of God, they did not speak of a mission of salvation to them. It should be observed that while Jonah
himself partakes of the older view of judgment, the author of the
book does not share that view. Behind the Book of Jonah lie the
experiences of the Exile and the missionary universalism of such
great preachers as the Second Isaiah (see such passages as 42:6;
49:6; 52:15; 56:1-8; 60:3; 66:18-19). Almost every thought of
Jonah can be paralleled in the series of messages in Isaiah 40-66.
But there is another element which must be taken into account
in connection with the growing vision of a universal mission.
With that broad conception of the power and concern of God
went an ever narrowing exclusivism, resulting in part from the
hard life experienced by those who had returned from the Exile,

as demonstrated in Haggai, Zechariah, Malachi, Ezra, and Nehemiah. Our author appears to carry forward the earlier and more humanitarian views of Second Isaiah as over against the attitude of the exclusivists of his day. But just exactly when he penned his thoughts cannot be determined more precisely. It was sometime between the end of the Exile and the beginning of the fourth century B.C.

Historical Situation

Of the historical situation we know absolutely nothing. We can only speculate about it on the basis of the foregoing observations. The references to the king of Nineveh, the size of the city, and its reaction to the preaching of Jonah are hardly historical (see discussion of passages involved), as other extant material indicates.

The Purpose

The Book of Jonah was a protest against the developing narrowness of the Jewish community after the Exile, and attempted to show the world-wide interest and concern of the Lord. The bitterness brought on by the Exile and the sufferings which the Jews who returned from Babylon experienced at the hands of foreign powers and interests had naturally generated a climate of resentment and a hope that God would intervene to wipe out the enemies of his people. Jonah himself is treated as representative of that hope.

In the first place he resents the mission to Nineveh, a foreign people at whose hands Israel had suffered much. Jonah did not share the broad view of the author, whose sentiments are those of the Lord (3:10; 4:11). Jonah was obviously of the same mind as Nahum, who rejoiced over the downfall of the ancient enemy in the celebrated poem recorded in the third chapter of his prophecy.

Jonah is presented as one who could not conceive of the Lord's forgiveness of Nineveh. For him, God was the God of Israel; and other peoples were, in Jonah's way of thinking, idolaters, who had no right to expect mercy or salvation at the hands of God.

Literary Form and Composition

The Book of Jonah differs from the other prophetic books in that it is not a collection of oracles delivered by a prophet but is a story about a prophet. As such it is like other stories in the Old Testament, for example, those about Elijah, Ruth, and Joseph. It is altogether possible that the author used the Elijah stories in the Books of Kings as his model. But having said this, one must go a step further and observe that the writer is not engaged in the production of a historical document; he has given us, rather, a parable, or perhaps a sermon, on the obligation of a prophet of the Lord.

To produce his parable the author drew upon a number of sources, though probably none was actually a written composition. First there was, of course, the historical person of Jonah, around whom the whole parable is composed. Then there was the psalm of thanksgiving which has been inserted between 2:1 and 2:10, and which itself contains numerous parallels with the Psalms. Finally there is the story of the fish, which has been responsible for all sorts of strained allegorical interpretations. There may also be some contact with the prophecy of Joel (for example, compare Jonah 3:9 with Joel 2:14, and Jonah 4:2 with Joel 2:13).

As it stands, the story seems to be a well-defined unit with the possible exception of the psalm, which, if left out, does not affect the thread of the story at all. Whether it was a part of the original is uncertain. The poetry of the psalm compares favorably with that of other psalms, and the prose of the story is excellent.

The Message

The message of Jonah is, in some respects, closer to that of the New Testament than that of any other book in the Old Testament. Much of the message of the book has already been given, but special attention may be called here to several specific points. First there is the emphasis upon the universal dominion of God. He has power over land and sea; he is the Creator of all, and all people command his interest. His grace, love, and forgiveness are as available for the sailors or the people of Nineveh as they are for Jonah and his people. Jonah is a standing rebuke to narrowness and exclusivism. It is a book of the universal love of God who is concerned about all people, and who stands ready to pardon and forgive all those who repent and call upon him in time of need.

Second, there is the willingness of foreigners to learn of the God of Israel and to respond to his offer to them. As such they are a striking contrast to the people who were his beneficiaries over the centuries but who failed to appreciate his Covenant of loyalty and refused to turn from their evil ways, though they were warned again and again.

Third, there is the obvious missionary motive involved in the Lord's commission to Jonah to preach to the pagan citizens of the great Assyrian metropolis. There was always a tendency among the Hebrews to regard God's election solely as conveying special privilege. But that was a complete misunderstanding of the election love of God. He chose them to be his servant, and laid upon them the obligation of informing the nations of God's concern for them and witnessing before them the meaning of his salvation. In the same way, the Lord who declared, "Something greater than Jonah is here" (Matt. 12:41), possibly warning against Christian exclusiveness, commanded his followers to "go . . . and make disciples of all nations" (Matt. 28:19).

OUTLINE

COMMENTARY

THE CALL AND FLIGHT OF JONAH
Jonah 1:1-16

The Call of Jonah (1:1-2)

The expression "the word of the LORD came" (1:1) is a normal introductory formula, indicating that revelation from the Lord has been received by his messenger or prophet. (Compare the introductory words of Hosea, Joel, Micah, Zephaniah, Haggai, Zechariah, and Jeremiah.) The revelation that came to Jonah is not specified beyond the direction to proceed to Nineveh and to cry against it because of its sinfulness. Something of the nature of that revelation may, however, be gathered from the simple proclamation recorded in 3:4. Of Jonah himself we know nothing except that he is probably to be identified with Jonah the son of Amittai from Gath-hepher in Galilee, who prophesied in the days of Jeroboam II (II Kings 14:25).

"Nineveh, that great city" (vs. 2) was the capital of Assyria and was located on the left bank of the Tigris River, some forty miles north of the greater Zab junction. The city was overthrown by the Medo-Babylonian army in 612 B.C. The peremptory order given by the Lord reminds us of the summons issued to Amos (7:15) to prophesy against Israel. Jonah was to proclaim or preach against Nineveh because of its great wickedness, which the Lord had observed. This command points to the prophetic conception of the Lord as the Ruler and Controller of all history, who had power over Nineveh just as he had over Jerusalem.

Jonah's Flight (1:3)

For some reason, not explained here (but see 4:2), Jonah decided to flee from the Lord. He did not yet understand the universal power or concern of the Lord, from whom no one could escape. In his urge to get away from the Lord he went down to Joppa (modern Jaffa), a seaport, to board a ship for "Tarshish," often identified with Tartessus in Spain, but more probably a place in Sardinia where there was a great iron smelter. If the latter interpretation is correct, Jonah bought passage on a commercial freighter which had brought iron or iron products to Palestine. In any event, Tarshish represents the farthest known distance from Palestine by sea, and Jonah wanted to get as far away from the Lord's land as possible, so as to avoid carrying out what to him was a distasteful mission whose success, from his point of view, was far from certain. The purpose of his act is stated twice in the verse—"to flee . . . from the presence of the LORD. . . . to go . . . away from the presence of the LORD" (vs. 3). Behind his action was the supposition that God was localized in his land, and confined to the area which he presumably controlled. Jonah thought that he could escape his task by leaving the land of the Lord.

The Storm (1:4-6)

But the Lord had other plans, with which Jonah had not reckoned. So the Lord of land and sea "hurled a great wind upon the sea" (vs. 4), so that the boat was about to be smashed by the huge waves. In their fear of the disaster, the sailors, tough as they doubtless were, cried each one to his god. They supported their prayers by direct action as "they threw the wares that were in the ship into the sea" (vs. 5). Obviously they hoped, by thus lightening the ship, to save it from being beaten to pieces. Jonah remained unworried, for he "had gone down into the inner part of the ship," where he lay down and fell asleep. He was apparently a happy man, comforted by the thought that he had outsmarted the Eternal; he was rapidly moving out of God's reach.

The captain of the ship was not so calm, because he knew the ways of the sea stirred up by storms. His deep concern is revealed by his sharp address to his passenger: "What do you mean, you sleeper?" The Hebrew word for "sleeper" in verse 6 describes one who is in a deep sleep, that is, in an unconcerned sleep. That seemed inexplicable to the captain in view of the dangerous situation, but it does emphasize the narrator's conception of the attitude of the prophet. The captain not only aroused Jonah, he urged him to wake up to the danger and call upon his god, as the members of the crew were doing, each to his own god. It may be of some significance that the pagan captain should demand prayer on the part of Jonah, the representative of the true God. The words "the god" are spoken from the captain's point of view, placing Jonah's God on the same level with pagan gods. The irony of the situation was that Jonah actually looked upon the Lord in the same narrow way.

Jonah and the Sailors (1:7-10)

Meanwhile the sailors had concocted a plan to discover by lot the one of their number responsible for the evil that had come upon them (vs. 7). The lot was commonly used in Israel to identify guilty persons (I Sam. 14:41-42) and to settle other matters (Num. 26:55; I Chron. 26:13). The lot came out for Jonah, who was immediately confronted with the results and questioned by the sailors. The first question had already been answered by the outcome of the casting of the lots, but either Jonah had not been informed of the outcome or they wanted to put the question directly. They continued their quest by inquiring about his occupation, his origin, his country, and his people—a rather thorough examination of the circumstances surrounding the activity of the man who was trying to run away from God.

As is customary in Hebrew narrative literature, there is here just enough material to provide the thread of the story. Much is left to the imagination of the reader. Hence the narrator presents only a very short response on the part of Jonah to the questions of the sailors. "I am a Hebrew" (vs. 9) tells us a great deal and answers the question about his origin and country. He also tells them that he is a worshiper of the Lord, "the God of heaven," which is a characterization favored by the late Hebrew writers in Persian times. The description of the Lord as the Creator of the sea and dry land is somewhat curious, in view of Jonah's attempt to get away from God, but it is expressive of the common Hebrew faith in the Lord as Creator of heaven and earth (see Gen. 1-2).

The reply of the prophet to the queries of the sailors struck consternation into their hearts, for they realized at once the cause of the calamity that had overtaken them—it was due to the Lord of land and sea. Their exclamation, "What is this that you have done!" points to their recognition of Jonah's disobedience (as the writer clearly indicates later in the verse); it also hints at more conversation between the prophet and the sailors than appears in his given response to their questions. Their fear was increased by the knowledge that they were the unsuspecting victims of the wrath of the God of heaven, earth, and sea.

A Sacrifice to the Sea (1:11-16)

Of course the first thing the sailors thought of was some way to quiet the raging sea and, since Jonah had told them that his God was the Lord of the dry land and the sea, they asked him what they should do with him "that the sea may quiet down" (vs. 11). The necessity of the moment was heightened because "the sea grew more and more tempestuous." There may be a subtle attempt on the part of the writer to place the pagan sailors in a favorable light as over against Jonah, whose desire for the destruction of the heathen is so conspicuous in chapter 4.

Jonah, knowing his guilt, was aware that nothing short of his removal would calm the angry sea. The sailors had requested an oracle on what to do (compare Acts 16:30) and he gave them the answer. To be saved they must cast him overboard as a kind of sacrifice to the sea. Here the prophet's sense of justice and righteousness comes into play in a worthy recognition of his own sin and a recommendation for making amends. The sailors were unwilling at first to take such drastic measures and stretched every sinew to bring the ship into port, but to no avail (vs. 13).

Before finally acceding to Jonah's advice to cast him overboard, the sailors called upon the God of Jonah in prayer, imploring him to save them and not to allow them to perish for the sake of "this man's life" (vs. 14). Since the storm was God's way of manifesting his displeasure at Jonah's act, let his will be done. The pagan sailors were, in effect, the agents who helped to carry out the will of the Lord, so that his message might be delivered to other pagans at Nineveh.

The simple act of throwing Jonah overboard is followed by the affirmation that then "the sea ceased from its raging" (vs. 15), and that "then the men feared the LORD exceedingly" (vs. 16). This may be considered as one of the striking lessons of the book. The conversion of these men was based on the saving grace and mercy of God. They had been thrown into a situation of near catastrophe, but out of that came a new experience of God, in gratitude for which they performed their act of worship —"they offered a sacrifice to the LORD and made vows" (compare Noah in Gen. 8:20). The vows doubtless involved a pledge to present other offerings when they got back to land once more, or to seek the Lord further at the earliest opportunity. The attitude of the sailors toward the Lord, and the fact that their sacrifices were apparently accepted—on a ship, away from the religious center of Jerusalem—demonstrate still more strongly the author's conception of the extent of the rule of God and the ac-

ceptability of the sacrifice of a broken and a contrite heart (Ps.
51:17) no matter where and by whom offered.

JONAH AND THE FISH
Jonah 1:17—2:10

Jonah Swallowed by the Fish (1:17)

Once again the story gives only sparse details in the progress
of Jonah's experience. It utilizes an ancient and widespread idea,
part of the popular literature of that and earlier days. The great
fish "appointed . . . to swallow up Jonah" is not intended to be
taken literally; it is the author's way of getting the prophet back
as quickly as possible to his task, and as such fits in quite well
with the story. God has a way of bringing his servants to a
speedy recognition of his will for them and of enforcing obedience thereto. Jesus' reference to the sign of Jonah (Matt. 12:39-
41; 16:4; Luke 11:29-32) has no bearing on the historicity of
the book or the literal character of the tale; it simply points to
knowledge of the story as it was told and retold in his time, just
as later some of his own parables were. The reference to the
three days is a kind of simile, drawing a comparison between the
story and Jesus' own experience. The *sign* of Jonah consists of
his proclamation to Nineveh (Luke 11:30) as a warning to repent before it is too late. So our Lord himself, in his call to repentance, is a sign to the people of his generation—a warning to
repent before destruction overtakes them.

The Prayer of Jonah (2:1, 10)

Chapter 2 begins with the announcement of a prayer of Jonah
"from the belly of the fish" (vs. 1), and ends with the statement
that the Lord spoke to the fish who then "vomited out Jonah
upon the dry land" (vs. 10). The prayer is not given but the context clearly indicates that Jonah besought the Lord for deliverance, and in so doing confessed his error, repented, and expressed his willingness to undertake the task the Lord had as-
signed to him in the beginning. Forgiveness and a new opportunity are granted the prophet just as readily as they were
granted to the repentant Ninevites later on. God demands obedience to
his will, but he is always ready to forgive those who are genuinely
sorry for their errors, repent, and express their willingness to
carry out his purpose.

A Psalm of Thanksgiving (2:2-9)

The tone of this passage is clear evidence that it is not the prayer uttered by Jonah in "the belly of the fish," though the author may have intended it to be his song of thanksgiving *after* deliverance. It is, however, generally regarded as an insertion into the original story, composed out of significant passages from several Psalms. There are a score or more similar individual songs of thanksgiving given in the Old Testament and the Apocrypha (for example, Pss. 18; 30; 32; 34; 40:2-12; 41; 66; 92; 116; 118; 138; Isa. 38:10-20; Job 33:26-28; Sirach 51; Tobit 13; The Prayer of Manasseh). Such psalms are generally characterized by petition, a rehearsal of the sin or illness which afflicted the psalmist, an appeal to the Lord, and reference to his favorable response. Interpreted in this light, Jonah's psalm of thanksgiving is a beautiful prayer coming from a significant experience in the poet's life.

Verse 2 is similar to expressions in Psalms 120:1; 18:5-6; 30:3. The tense of the verbs points to a time past when the writer called upon the Lord for help. He was then in distress of some kind—illness, oppression, or even shipwreck. Whatever it was, it was very real because of the terms used to describe it— "the belly of Sheol." This phrase in the psalm probably accounts for its presence in the present context in Jonah. "Sheol" is often used metaphorically for the deepest distress or severest affliction. In such a condition the psalmist found consolation in the Lord who heard his cry and answered it by deliverance.

Verse 3 is a further description of the travail in which the writer found himself when he called upon the Lord. The Lord had brought on his distress but he had also delivered him (see Job 5:18; Isa. 19:22; 30:26; Hosea 6:1). The "heart of the seas" is a metaphor for the depth of the trouble, as are the succeeding parallels, "the flood was round about me" and "all thy waves and thy billows passed over me" (see Ps. 42:7).

Verse 4 reflects the time when he came to himself (see Luke 15:17), when he realized that he was an outcast, far away from the Temple and the presence of God. He understood then what it meant to be left alone, to be the victim of his own follies, in a strange place away from the protection and blessing of God's presence. He had the same experience as the writer of Psalm 42 who, in his time of exile, also longed ardently for the presence of the Lord and for participation in the services of his Temple.

Verses 5 and 6 form a repetition, in general, of verse 3. "The waters closed in" over him, and "the deep" surrounded him on all sides. The seaweeds entangled themselves around him (the Hebrew word is used for the reeds of the Nile, Exod. 2:3, 5; Isa. 19:6). Then the figure changes, and the psalmist thinks of himself as descending into the clefts of the mountains where the "bars" of the land threatened to envelop him. He thus compares himself with one about to be swallowed up by the sea or enclosed forever in the bowels of the earth. The Revised Standard Version interprets the passage slightly differently, as it takes the first phrase of verse 6 with the preceding clause, and has the roots of the mountains extending into the subterranean waters, upon which they were thought to float. But that requires a change of the text which seems unnecessary, however attractive. It appears better to interpret as indicated above, in which case verse 6 would read:

> I went down into the clefts of the mountains,
> The earth with its bars (was) about me forever.

Both figures are explained in the last line of verse 6: "thou didst bring up my life from the Pit." The term "Pit" is the regular word in Semitic literature for the realm of the dead. The writer affirms that the Lord had snatched him from the jaws of death, delivering him before the gates of Sheol closed upon him. Sheol was the land of no return.

When he was about to be engulfed, the psalmist remembered the Lord and resorted to prayer (vs. 7). His prayer ascended to God in his holy Temple, his earthly residence or dwelling place. The response to this prayer is not stated, but the song of thanksgiving is ample evidence that it was favorable.

The writer's experience demonstrated the Lord's loyalty (mercy), even in the most trying circumstances (vs. 8). He had seen others appealing "to vain idols," all to no avail. Whatever else he may have learned, the psalmist now understood clearly that the Lord alone heard prayer and had the power of salvation.

The great deliverance which the psalmist had experienced led him to offer sacrifices of thanksgiving to the Lord, not only on this occasion but throughout his life (vs. 9). Thanksgiving is always an outgrowth of joy attendant upon the reception of a precious gift. He had received such a gift and hence paid his vow in

thanksgiving as others had in like experiences (Gen. 28:20; I
Sam. 1:11; Job 22:27; Ps. 50:14, 23).

JONAH'S SECOND CALL AND RESPONSE
Jonah 3:1-10

The Second Call (3:1-2)

The issuance of a second call is not customary in the case of
the other prophets, whose call was always regarded as extremely
urgent. The writer here may be thinking of something more than
Jonah and his mission to Nineveh. Without the qualification of
"the second time," the commission could equally well be the
first, for its wording is quite similar; the only difference is in the
second half of verse 2 where "proclaim to it the message that I
tell you" appears in place of "for their wickedness has come up
before me" (1:2). Since Jonah is to be viewed as a likeness of
Israel, the messenger or servant of the Lord, it may be that here
there is offered to the nation a second chance. The Jews had been
brought back from Babylon, and had been reinvested with the
Lord's commission to proclaim his message of salvation to all
nations. More than one prophet's call included a responsibility for
the nations (see Jer. 1:5; Isa. 49:6). Could the writer of our book
be thinking of the Servant passage just noted (Isa. 49:6)? This
was Jonah's second opportunity and he was urged to present to
the Ninevites "the message" that God would give him at the moment of delivery.

The Response of Jonah (3:3-4)

Once more details are lacking. We are not told how Jonah got
to his destination, how long it took him to get there, or any experiences he may have had on the way. These are left to the imagination of the reader. All that is said is that "Jonah arose and
went to Nineveh, according to the word of the LORD" (vs. 3).
This, too, may have been a part of his thanksgiving for the deliverance he enjoyed at the hands of the Lord. The writer of the
song of thanksgiving spoke of the paying of his vow (2:9); perhaps Jonah also made a vow that, if delivered, he would henceforth carry out the Lord's mission, and when the call came a second time he made haste to fulfill it. The greatness of the city, as
well as the number and character of the inhabitants, must have

given him pause. The description, "three days' journey in breadth," appears to be a tremendous exaggeration, intended to explain the previous reference to it as an "exceedingly great city." Perhaps the author, influenced by Genesis 10:11-12, had in mind Assyria or a much larger district or metropolis, of which Nineveh was the center; for example, the triangular district of Khorsabad, Nineveh, and Nimrud (Kalhu). Diodorus Siculus says the wall of Nineveh measured 480 stadia (some 60 miles). But the ruins of the walls are only about seven and a half miles in circumference. This is another strong argument against the historicity of the book, unless "Nineveh" is to be identified as "Assyria." "A day's journey" into the city would be about 25 miles, an obviously fantastic figure. What the author means is that the job of Jonah was very great, and the world to which he was sent was populous and extensive. But Jonah undertook it, though with misgivings, as is evident later. As he went he proclaimed the message that God had taken note of the wickedness of the city, and cried, "Yet forty days, and Nineveh shall be overthrown!" (vs. 4).

The Repentance of the City (3:5)

The response to the proclamation of Jonah was electric. What the other prophets had hoped for in vain when they announced the oracles of the Lord (Isaiah, Hosea, Jeremiah), Jonah achieved among this foreign people. For "the people of Nineveh believed [in] God" (vs. 5), and as an expression of the sincerity of their repentance they fasted and "put on sackcloth." Here is manifestly one of the serious lessons of the book—the willingness of the heathen to listen to the appeal of God, as over against the stubbornness and callousness of Israel. This is seen also in the obedience of the people of Nineveh to the word of the Lord in contrast to the disobedience of Jonah himself.

The Reaction of the King (3:6-9)

The reaction of the "king of Nineveh" also offers a welcome contrast to that of some kings of Israel and Judah to the preaching of the other prophets. The reference to the "king of Nineveh" is another indication of the nonhistorical character of the book, for nowhere else is the king of Assyria so named. The concern of the author is not history, but the proclamation of the word of the Lord to all peoples, even the people of Assyria. The king himself joined in the fast and mourning as soon as he was informed of the threat announced by Jonah. Not only so, but he and his officials issued a decree enjoining fasting, the donning of sackcloth, and intercession with God. The inclusion of animals is a descriptive figure, indicating total humiliation, but it must be remembered that in the Old Testament God cares for the animals as well as for men (see Pss. 50:10; 104:10-30; 145:15). The proclamation of decrees was common in the Persian period, and those recorded in the Bible (Ezra 1:1-4; 6:1-12) are in the same general form as this one. The king was not satisfied with mere external humiliation; the people must "cry mightily to God" and everyone must "turn from his evil way and from the violence which is in his hands" (vs. 8). Repentance requires more than sackcloth, fasting, and sitting in the dust; to be sincere and serious it requires a change of life and perspective. What a lesson this must have been to Jonah and his fellow Jews! He learned more from the Ninevites than he taught them.

Verse 9 emphasizes the fact that forgiveness and salvation are not won by outward ceremonies of religion or observances of days of humiliation, but are the gifts of God's love and grace.

The Gift of God (3:10)

In view of their faith in God, their response to his word delivered by the prophet, and their honest repentance, the Ninevites were spared. God did not carry out his threat to destroy them. Here is another great lesson of our book. The word of the Lord not only went out to the heathen Ninevites but it was believed by them, even though there was no extensive campaign of religious instruction to prepare them for it. God did for the repentant Ninevites what he was prevented from doing for his Chosen People because of their unbelief and disobedience. No people on earth is beyond the concern of God (see Matt. 28:19-20), or beyond the possibility of faith and repentance and salvation. Conversely, there are no limits to the grace and mercy of God; they are not confined to Israel or even to Christians, but are operative to all who believe and are truly sorry for their sins. To be faced with this truth must have been a terrific blow to those proud Israelites who looked upon themselves as alone having access to the throne of the Eternal. And it is meant to be a rebuke to their exclusiveness, and to ours.

THE REACTION OF JONAH
Jonah 4:1-5

From the point of view of the law of his people, Jonah had every right to be profoundly disturbed, for according to Deuteronomy 18:22 the very reputation of the prophet depended on the fulfillment of his prophecy. In fact, Jonah could actually be accused of being a false prophet, for his prophecy did not come to pass. Here was a case in which a prophet succeeded in proportion as his prediction failed. It was not the Lord's purpose, of course, to destroy even Nineveh; his purpose was to save it. Prophecy was directed to the salvation of the people, and so the prophetic word was always somewhat conditional—if the people repented, destruction would be stayed; if not, it would come to pass.

The whole experience brought forth a prayer of bitter complaint, reproaching the Lord for his act of forgiveness and reminding him of what had transpired between himself and Jonah before the prophet's attempt to escape to Tarshish (vs. 2). Apparently more had happened then than appears in chapter 1. His prayer refers to this in an attempt at self-justification. What he predicted for Nineveh did not come to pass because the Lord is "a gracious God and merciful, slow to anger, and abounding in steadfast love," and repents of evil (vs. 2). This is one of the greatest passages of the Bible, first uttered by the Lord himself to Moses (Exod. 34:6). Jonah objected to it as applying to others outside his own nation. On the other hand, he knew that "steadfast love" ("loyalty," a Covenantal term) was one of the chief characteristics of the Lord, and that his Covenantal offer went back to the time of Noah when the Lord promised never again to destroy the world with a flood (Gen. 9:8-17). As he observed, the Lord exercised his mercy and fulfilled his Covenant promise by saving the repentant Ninevites, which should have pleased the prophet rather than upset him. It should have taught him the magnitude and glory of the God he served, but he wanted to restrict God and his saving love to himself and his people.

Jonah thought he had failed and would be the object of ridicule. In his despondency he prayed the Lord to take his life, as Moses (Num. 11:15) and Elijah (I Kings 19:4) had done. Elijah's message had failed to convert his people; Jonah's had been eminently successful in bringing about repentance, but he believed himself discredited because of his narrow conception of God. He could not face the broader idea of God involved in the "success" of his mission. The word of the Lord appears not to have had any effect on Jonah. God's question, "Do you do well to be angry?" was an invitation to consider his point of view and with it Jonah's whole theology. Such was the answer of the Lord to the prophet's prayer.

Seeing the signs of Nineveh's repentance, Jonah still could not believe his eyes. Had not God, after all, sent him to say, "Yet forty days . . . "? Surely the repentance of these wicked people had temporarily hoodwinked the Lord and he will yet act to carry out his word! So Jonah left the city, journeyed a short distance to the east—perhaps to an eminence, where he made a booth for protection from the sun by day and the chill by night —and sat down to see what would happen. Thirty-seven days was a long time to wait!

THE LORD'S LESSON TO JONAH
Jonah 4:6-11

The Lord caused "a plant . . . [to] come up over Jonah, that it might be a shade over his head, to save him from his discomfort" (vs. 6). The sudden appearance of the plant, sufficiently large to enable a man to sit under it, points again to the nonhistorical character of the story, and has no significance for the lesson involved. As Jonah had been graciously delivered from a watery grave by the Lord, so once more he finds himself in his beneficent hands, this time being afforded the shade of a plant to protect him from the direct rays of the sun, and thus being saved from possible sunstroke. He was most happy and grateful for the provision of the Lord, as he had been for deliverance from the sea. He rejoiced and was thankful for God's grace so wondrously granted him twice. Such appreciation on his part should have awakened his thoughts to the situation of the Ninevites, whose gratitude was expressed in their repentance, alteration of life, and faith in the Lord. How much joy there must have been in their hearts! God had cared for them.

Jonah's joy was short-lived, for the next day a worm bored through the heart of the plant so that it withered and died. Thus the plant which had come up so suddenly vanished just as suddenly, and with it went the prophet's protection. There, in the heat of the blazing Assyrian sun, was a vivid lesson in the meaning of destruction, whose import Jonah utterly failed to grasp. For, when the hot east wind arose that day, the plant dried up; the heat of the sun beat down upon his head, and Jonah became faint. Once more he asked that he might die. Again the Lord puts to him the question, "Do you do well to be angry . . . ?" (vs. 9). The earlier response of Jonah was to wait in the hope that he might yet see the literal fulfillment of his prediction; but this time it is an audible response: "I do well to be angry, angry enough to die."

The last two verses make the application of the lesson for Jonah. He had pity upon the plant, with whose sprouting and growth he had nothing to do, and whose span of life was so short. "Should not I," asked the Lord, "pity Nineveh . . . ?" The sympathy of the prophet for the plant was not matched by pity for the great city with its teeming population of persons. Yet he had not even had a hand in the growth of the plant, while the Lord did have something to do with Nineveh. He was its Creator and, therefore, stood in a real relationship to its people. Here were "a hundred and twenty thousand persons who do not know their right hand from their left, and also much cattle." The reference is to the children, and does not include the adults. It has been estimated that Nineveh could have had a population of 174,000 persons. A recently discovered inscription of Asshurnasirpal II (883-859 B.C.) tells of a banquet with a total of 69,574 invited guests. Taking into account the surrounding population and the foreigners, the figures given here in Jonah do not appear so fantastic as is sometimes thought. But the essence of the declaration does not lie in the exact figures or in its historical accuracy; it lies rather in the mercy of the Lord extended to repentant Nineveh, whose people were his children just as really as were those of Judah, yet did not have the religious advantages of the latter. Jonah was thus led by personal experience, somewhat as Hosea had been, to an understanding of the nature of God. And there the story ends, pointing to the writer's faith in the operation of the grace and mercy of God for all the world, in contradistinction to the narrowness and exclusiveness of postexilic Judaism which tended to confine them to the elect. Jonah is the book of the universal grace of God and, as such, is the first great missionary tract of the Bible.